Winning Relationships

By the same author

Women and Stress
Men and Stress
Teenagers and Stress

Winning Relationships

Dr Charmaine Saunders

MILNER HEALTH SERIES

First published in 2001 by
Sally Milner Publishing Pty Ltd
PO Box 2104
Bowral NSW 2576
AUSTRALIA

©DR CHARMAINE SAUNDERS

Design by Anna Warren
Typeset by Sandra Goldbloom Zurbo
Editing by Sandra Goldbloom Zurbo

Printed in Australia

National Library of Australia Cataloguing-in-Publication data:
　Saunders, Charmaine.
　　Winning relationships.

　　Bibliography
　　ISBN 1 86351 291 8.

　　1. Interpersonal relations. 2. Communication. 3. Stress management. I. Title.

　158.2

All rights reserved. No part of this publication may be reproduced; stored in a retrieval system or transmitted in any form or by any means, electronic, mechanical, photocopying, recording or otherwise, without prior written permissions of the copyright holders.

Dedication

This book is dedicated to all the people I've had relationships with in my life—friends, lovers, family, colleagues, students, readers and clients, especially those who have hurt and disappointed me because they have taught me most of all.

A special dedication to my second mother, Erla, who died last year. More than anyone, she encouraged me to write and was always proud of me before I knew there was anything to be proud of. I will always miss you.

Contents

	Acknowledgements	ix
	Introduction	xi
1.	The Nature of Stress	1
2.	Relationship Stress	27
3.	The Nature of Relationships	53
4.	Relationship History	77
5.	Communication	95
6.	Before and After Relationships	115
7.	Relationship With Self	139
	References	163

Acknowledgements

My partner, Chris, has helped me give myself more freely and fearlessly to love because now I feel I am in a safe harbour. Coco, my irascible, adorable, bossy and eternally playful chinchilla cat, keeps me ever-mindful of the importance of fun and keeps me connected to my inner child—a rare and special gift.

My mother has given me many gifts, including the gift of her imperfection which has taught me a lot and made me strong.

My brother Michael and my sister Sharon filled the places in my heart where the children I couldn't have should have been.

My aunts, uncles and cousins who I have loved since childhood, and my many friends who mean so much to me that my life would be quite empty without them—you know who you are and how much I love you.

Each of my partners, who both loved me and hurt me—without them, I could never have learnt so much about myself, healed my emotional wounds and become who I am today.

My work colleagues who help and support me so much, in particular, Grayam Howells and Sue Dupereusel of the Life Centre, Tony Flursheim of Agora Marketing, Jon Hanlin and Peter Gibbons of Healthlife, everyone at the Claremont Medical Centre, Tamara Pitelen at 'B', Hazel Bradley and Sandy Mcphie at 'For Me', Karen Reynolds and Liz Tilly at UWA extension, Jill

Rogers at radio station 3AK Melbourne, Radio 6PR in Perth, my publisher, Libby Renney, and my editor, Sandra Goldbloom Zurbo.

Introduction

THIS BOOK IS ABOUT WINNING relationships. That doesn't mean you'll always have relationships that are only easy, stress-free and continually joyful. What it does mean is that you can have relationships that are real, healthy and rewarding. My aim is to help you to understand how stress works in your life, what relationships mean and how you can change your life for the better.

This is my sixth book. Four of the previous five are about stress. Does this mean I am a placid and relaxed person? No! I have had to fight the desire to stress out all my life, so the techniques and advice I offer are from first-hand experience. Everything in my work is about positive change and practical self-help.

I believe that each one of us has the power and strength to be happy and successful; what I provide is the 'how to' part.

The chief aim of this book is to provide a blueprint with which you can take an honest look at yourself, the way you're living your life and the quality of your relationships. The tools I offer are applicable to all your relationships, not just the close personal ones. Each one of us experiences many relationships as we go through a lifetime—some casual, some intense, some joyful, some painful. There are people in our lives who seem to bring us only pleasure, while others continually press our buttons and force us to confront our lessons. Both are equally valuable.

In matters of love and the human heart, we are all seekers. We've all been hurt and we've all hurt others. The more we learn and grow, the less we feel the pain of loneliness, isolation, regret, sadness, anxiety and conflict.

Many of my readers over the past fifteen years have written to me with feedback; it's one of the greatest gifts of my life You are encouraged to write to me about your life, your story and experiences. I can be contacted at Box 637, Subiaco, Western Australia 6904, or email me at <dearchar@hotmail.com>. My phone number is 61 (0)8 9487 3014 (international callers leave the zero off the 08). Writing is a lonely occupation but knowing that people all over the world will read and benefit from my thoughts and words makes it all worthwhile.

I have written this book with love and joy, as I try to do everything. I hope you will have the same feelings reading it.

The more motivated you are to work through the ideas and suggestions contained within the pages of this book, the greater will be your transformation and progress. I wish you all that and much more. Travel this journey with me.

1.
The Nature of Stress

WE HEAR SO MUCH ABOUT stress today. But is stress really a phenomenon of the late twentieth century, or has it always been around and we simply make more of a fuss about it than did our predecessors? Certainly, we can create even more stress by focusing on it too much, yet the truth is that stress is not a bad thing. Stress only becomes 'bad' if we allow ourselves to live with too much of it or if we handle it poorly.

Stress is in itself necessary and even helpful to human life. The problems start when we get hooked on the negative effects of stress, such as pressure, rushing, anger, frustration, overachieving, obsessiveness, workaholism, perfectionism and control. These will all be looked at in later chapters but my plan is to examine in this first chapter some of the general issues surrounding stress before we apply them to the specific area of relationships.

Let's face it, some of us are natural stress-merchants who are easily harassed and want everything done yesterday and perfectly, while others can come face to face with a howling hurricane and shrug philosophically. It comes with the genes and, while our basic natures are about the only thing we cannot change, the very fact of our awareness enables us to modify our behaviour and make healthy adjustments. For example, if you know that you're a naturally stressful person, you might want to adapt your lifestyle to suit your temperament. Some people get stressed if they have too much to do so cut back on non-essentials. Others have highly pressurised jobs so they have to learn to delegate where possible and practise letting go at the end of the workday. Yet others have a lot of personal obligations and testing relationships; here, the skills of assertiveness and setting healthy boundaries will help a lot.

Knowledge is power so find out about yourself first and then plan around that. Also allow for family conditioning because if you came from a family background where stress was the norm, it's quite likely that you will fall into the same trap. Identify your particular stress trap and change that first. It could be your job—is it wrong for you? do you have to work under stressful conditions? have you got a difficult boss or unpleasant coworkers? are the hours too long? do you have to travel a long way to get to work?

Is it your health? Health problems are a pretty accurate gauge of stress levels—long before you realise you're in stress overload, your body will start to break down in small or big ways, depending on your general fitness. Is it your home or neighbourhood?

Is it your mental attitude and psychological state? Finally, is it your relationships, close or otherwise?

Even if you are not naturally stressful, just the fact that you're alive at this time in history will cause you stress. We may not have discovered stress but we have certainly found many ways to make it far more complex and damaging. Instead of it working for us, it then works against us, and by far the most destructive factor about chronic stress is its insidious, subtle nature. It has a seductive quality that offers pleasure while it's hurting, makes you high while you're absorbing all its negative energies. I make it sound almost human, don't I? Well, stress is highly personal and it's comparable to the effect drugs have on addicts. It feels like your best friend but, in reality, it's robbing you of all discernment and discrimination.

It's the ongoing, habitual stress you need to beware of, not the occasional burst of pressure that happens to everyone from time to time. This is due to the reasons I mentioned in the previous paragraph: before you even notice the harm it's doing, once it gets hold of you, you can be hooked for a long time—then you have to release yourself from its hold on you in the same way as you do with any other addiction.

I advocate prevention. All of my work with stress—in books such as this one, or in classes and workshops or on radio and television—is about education for stress management as part of an overall lifestyle.

The first step is total honesty with yourself and taking stock of the stress in your life. If you feel that you are living with acceptable levels of stress, then look at the people, situations and events around you. Are they being experienced at comfortable levels? Armed with honest answers to this question, you can make a plan of action that's realistic and relatively easy. If your stress management plan is hard work, you've simply created another stress for yourself instead of alleviating pressure. Identify your main stress area and think of simple ways to moderate the problem. Sometimes a radical approach is required, as in the case of being in the wrong job. It may very well be necessary to leave employment that is affecting your health.

To help you decide if your stress levels are reasonable, look at these lists of some common stress symptoms and check off those you suffer from.

Physical

chronic fatigue
chronic insomnia
inexplicable aches and pains
constant headaches
lethargy
low immunity to infection
skin irritation

Mental

poor concentration
confusion
disorientation
inefficiency
memory loss

Emotional

joylessness
mood swings
loss of libido
breakdown of key relationships

If you feel that you are displaying several of these symptoms, do not panic. Even a lifelong stress habit can be redressed.

> **Here's what I suggest you do**
> - Take a long, hard look at your overall lifestyle.
> - Identify your particular stress trap.
> - Write down some small ways in which you can make positive improvements.
> - Commit to a more balanced way of life.
>
> **Let's take each of these in turn.**

Stress management is essentially life management

We each have 24 hours a day to live and adults have the choice of how to structure and spend those hours. It always amuses me when people say to me, 'But there aren't enough hours in a day.' What would be enough? Busy people would say they need unlimited time and depressed people would say a day feels as long as ten years. It's all relative and, in many ways, a rationalisation for not getting things done. The secret is to use the 24 hours each day in a balanced way; too much control is as bad as none. I prefer to use the word 'manage' as it is gentler and less rigid than 'control'.

Balance is certainly a key factor, as is time management. So, in examining your current lifestyle, look at all its aspects—diet, exercise, sleep, relaxation, relationships, work, money, home and any other details that relate to daily living. If you're ruthlessly honest, you will very quickly identify your weak spot and that leads to point 2.

Letting a relationship go

If your stress trap turns out to be a key relationship, you have to either let this person go out of your life or change your interaction pattern. This is much more difficult than if it's your old clanger of a car you have to get rid of or changing the suburb you live in or leaving an unsuitable job—these are relatively easy situations to change. But, whatever it is, you must take the bull by the horns—it won't ever get better by itself; it can only ever get worse.

Next, apart from whatever attitudinal changes or radical alterations you may be prepared to make, there is a whole range of smaller adjustments which, in themselves, once enacted, will immediately make life more comfortable. Write down the easy ones first and start working on them straight away. The success you witness will give you the encouragement for the next, more difficult stage.

Let me share a case study with you, one that will make this clearer.

I had a client who consulted me for extreme stress that was, she said, coming from her job, which, in turn, was affecting her relationship at home with her de facto husband. I advised her to think about changing jobs as that seemed to be the source of most of her aggravation. After the consultation, the woman had to go interstate and it was some weeks before I saw her again. When she walked in, she looked relaxed and glowing. It was a new job that had changed her, she said, and then proceeded to tell me the details. Finally, I asked her how her relationship was going, hoping she would report an improvement now that the job stress was removed. Instead, she announced brightly, 'Oh, I ended that.' The removal of one stress had highlighted the separate existence of another, which appeared to be caused by the original but in fact was destructive in its own right.

My own struggle with stress spanned many years and grew from pressure to overachieve, self-esteem that was tied to my output and accomplishments, and a deep-seated desire to gain my mother's approval. It may be appropriate in the course of writing this book to share some details of these issues but for the purpose of this introductory chapter, let me just say that I was not aware of having a stress problem as such. I thought I was simply a perfectionist, a hard-working, determined woman with a type A personality. Until things got so bad that I was forced to take stock and reshape my life, I never associated my chronic ill-health with the amount of stress I lived with and took for granted. One of my objectives in writing books about stress is to help people like the me I used to be to recognise much sooner if they're living with lethal levels of stress.

Why wait for a serious disease or a relationship breakdown to alert you to the hazards of your lifestyle? Last week, I asked a client to describe a typical day in her life. I was horrified—it was oh, so familiar. I suggested that she had a busyness addiction and she readily agreed.

It's not enough to simply change the practical details—

rearranging schedules, cutting out unnecessary items, getting more help, doing less or such like—it is crucial to identify the reason for the stress addiction in the first place.

> low self-esteem
> loneliness
> excessive work ethic
> workaholism
> patterns from childhood
> praise-seeking
> excessive desire to please/help others
> identifying with output
> fear of mortality
> self-defeating behaviour
> negative labels

Some possible causes of stress

These points will be covered in following chapters but try for now to let your mind explore the reason or reasons for your need to overfill your plate if, in fact, this applies to you.

Let's take a sample day and look at some of the practical considerations that can make a big difference.

Morning
Many people wake feeling anxious, often a legacy from childhood fears and problems ranging from parental pressures

to hating school. To combat this feeling, start the day with some positive affirmations such as 'This is a perfect day', or 'I greet this day with joy'.

Try not to leap straight out of bed and race around before leaving for work, school, appointments or whatever. Even if you have to set the alarm for a few minutes earlier, it's worth it to give yourself a slower start. People wake up differently in the morning: some instantly and brightly, some slowly and grumpily. Allow yourself to do what feels right for you and respect your bed partner's wishes if you have one. Nothing is worse than starting the day with a row.

Always eat breakfast, even if it's very, very light, and sit quietly to do it. Music or morning television is fine. The most important factor in a household at breakfast time is order, a system. If everything is left to chance, particularly if you have children, chaos will reign and you'll have a headache before you've even begun your working day.

No matter what your specific living arrangements, try to keep to a rough plan in regards to time and who does what. If you are the parent or someone otherwise in charge, don't be afraid to delegate—get as much help as you can. People are always more important than things so leave the dirty dishes if it means spending a few precious moments more with a child or a spouse before you go your separate ways.

The working day

Throughout the day, make sure you take sufficient breaks, especially over lunch, which should never be eaten at the desk or in a hurry. If you have appointments all day, schedule them with breaks in between to allow for overlapping or delays; if there is no overlapping or any delays, then you'll have given yourself the bonus of a short rest between appointments.

The unexpected creates stress—allow for various contingencies without being overly rigid. Worrying about things going wrong is stressful; planning ahead with time to spare is stress management. If you start feeling tired or edgy, walk around for a while or do some deep breathing and/or stretching at your desk. Deal with workplace irritations or hassles in a calm, assertive manner, not personally or emotionally.

Most important of all, when you've finished working for the day, whether it be five in the evening, eight o'clock at night or midnight, you must finish altogether. Taking work home is a big no-no, as are dealing with work issues in the evening, phoning about work and thinking about work. You are not really relaxed if only your body is; your mind also needs to let go. More about this in the next section on stress management techniques.

Returning home

The hours between four in the afternoon and seven at night are, potentially, the most stressful in any household so I recommend to everyone that it's best to do only what must be done and no more. It is not the time for visitors, phone calls, disciplining, deep talks or tantrums. You can have your nervous breakdown when the mad hour is over.

One woman with young children told me that she used to dread this time of day until she got the brainwave of hiding in her room from four to six every afternoon. I pronounced her a brave woman indeed, but she said it was very successful. Her children accepted that she wasn't available at these hours and they adapted, even to the point of sorting out their own disputes.

This might be more radical a step than you're ready to adopt but you could always try a modified version. Whatever you do, keep it simple; again, have a regular routine so the children know what their boundaries are. There's no point letting them run amuck and then complaining when your patience runs out.

In terms of your adult relationship, it's important to have quality time every day, not now and again or on weekends only. Quality time may take the form of watching television together, sitting quietly and talking or listening to music, or making an early night of it. It doesn't matter. If you are not with a partner, the same principle applies—cut off from work in a definite way and then relax with an activity you enjoy. Socialising is good, but remember—balance. Going out every night to alleviate boredom or loneliness will create pressures in other areas, but staying home all the time is not desirable either.

Sleep is a vital stress-management tool. If you're not sleeping enough or well, everything you need to do during the day will start to feel more burdensome. So, prepare yourself for quality sleep. Relax long before you get into bed, make your bedroom into an environment of peace and harmony and try to get into a regular pattern for sleeping.

Chronic insomnia is a telltale sign of stress overload which, in turn, creates further stress.

Some quick suggestions for insomnia are relaxation tapes, meditation, chamomile tea or warm milk, light, soothing exercise, reading or soft music.

Two practices to avoid completely are lying in bed thinking about work or problems and hassling in the bedroom about anything. If you are having a disagreement with your partner, never try to sort it out in bed as bed should always be your haven at the end of the day. If you develop this attitude of bed as a haven, you will never get into bad sleeping habits.

I hope this sample plan of a typical day offers you a blueprint for a starting point. Some days simply won't go to plan, others are, of necessity, more filled up, and then there is always the unexpected. But, as long as these are in the minority, you'll cope. If all your days are chaotic and disorganised, your life will soon become just one long blur of pressure.

What should I do?

Okay, assuming you have recognised that you are now in stress overload, what to do?

Awareness is the first, all-important step. Next is having a plan. Identify your key stress trap and start there. Write down all the things that you believe are causing you the most stress at the moment. Pick one to start working on. It may be time management or the way you're spending your days; it may be something as obvious as a difficult job or boss; it may be something more crucial, such as the way you're acting in a relationship. A negative situation causes stress which, in turn, makes the situation worse, so stress has a circular effect. That's why it rarely gets better on its own. You have to make a conscious choice to change.

Some people can work alone, others need help and support. Depending on how serious your problem is, you can choose whether to reach out for a self-help book like this one, join a group or get individual counselling. Third-party advice is often very valuable for couples, as mediation removes the blame factor, cools the emotions and allows for rational thought. Options become clearer, enabling you to work on the issues together instead of fighting. Even if you ultimately break up, you will have gained valuable insights into your relationship and the inherent stresses.

Here are some general stress management techniques that will benefit you whatever your stresses and whether you're married, have a partner or are single, live alone, have a family or share a home.

Mechanical cut-off from work

It's important to trick yourself at the end of the working day by means of a procedure that signifies a cut-off, for instance, by changing out of work clothes, having a shower or bath, sitting down with a cup of tea or spending some time in the garden. The amount of cut-off time is less significant than the cut-off itself. After all, some of you are shift workers, some work odd hours; not everyone puts in a nine to five day.

If you go out to a job, the time for cut-off is when you arrive home. It's okay to talk briefly about your day, but avoid prolonged discussions; any obligatory homework should be done quickly and then put out of sight.

If you work from home or are self-employed, cutting off requires far more discipline but is even more essential. Use an answering machine after a set hour so that you're not at the mercy of inconsiderate clients. Deal with paperwork quickly, tidy up the day's loose ends, plan tomorrow, shut the door firmly on the workroom and switch off mentally—the hardest part. It's all a matter of attitude and once again, planning.

Cushions of time during the day for breathers

Whatever you do for a living—indoors or outdoors, working for yourself or a company—you can pace yourself so that everything gets done without a panic. Planning work commitments is the key. Tools such as lists, diaries and files are invaluable as long as they don't take over and cause you more rather than less stress. I used to be a compulsive list-maker, but keeping up with my lists took more time than just getting on with the jobs at hand. Prioritising is essential so that, at the end of the day, you've finished all the main tasks: anything else you get done after that is a bonus.

Don't line up appointments back to back and don't take on more than you can realistically manage that day. It's better to do a set number of things well than a whole lot of things badly, or left half-finished. Sloppy work habits are responsible for a lot of stress; this applies just as much in the home as it does at outside work. A neat work centre is also helpful; time wasted looking for things can be utilised more profitably.

I'm not suggesting that you work to a rigid time schedule. In fact, the better organised you are, the easier work becomes: efficiency frees up more time.

Isolate people and things that aggravate stress levels

Apart from lifestyle and time management, look at your relationships and habitual behaviours. Is there anything that could be altered to create less stress? You can't get rid of everyone you don't get along with, pick and choose your neighbours and workmates or modify your family's behaviours to suit yourself, so what's left?

Change your attitude from negative to positive. That's all you have control over so shift gears on the things that annoy you—you might be quite surprised at the result. If, for example, there's something about one of your children's behaviour that really irritates you, try approaching it from a different angle. If it's a relatively small thing, such as the way the child wears his hair, let it go; if it's more serious, such as drug-taking, try approaching it unemotionally; you are likely to see more desirable results and have a better rapport with your child than you otherwise would have.

Life's too short to stress over every little thing: though others can stress you, only you have the power to turn it from a negative to a positive force. So many people say that a crisis in the family forced everyone to communicate better and pull together.

Why wait for a crisis? Do it straight away and reap the benefits.

Exercise

Regular exercise is an excellent alleviator of stress as it reduces tension in an ongoing way. You can't separate your various components—fitness of the body will benefit well-being of the mind and this in turn will create emotional harmony—it's all interconnected. If you ignore one part, the rest will suffer.

In particularly stressful times, it's even more important to keep up physical exercise. When people say they're too busy to exercise they've got it a bit back-to-front. Exercising doesn't have to be formalised or heavy but it should be regular and, if possible, enjoyable as you're much more likely to keep it up if you find it pleasurable.

I don't believe in the 'no pain, no gain' philosophy: I think things should be easy as possible. Effort is not the same as struggle. Physical exertion is particularly effective for anger management—it's far better to throw a pillow than hit a person. When you feel angry, impatient or frustrated, run around the block a few times, lift some weights or hit a punching bag, then, when you've calmed down, deal with the problem.

Awareness of your needs and priorities

Being clear on what your personal needs are and being able to state them in a non-confronting way, as well as not being a martyr or a victim, is very important because if you keep subjugating yourself, the resentment that builds up over time eventually becomes explosive. Human beings have a number of everyday needs that have to be satisfied to a lesser or greater degree—physical, emotional, sexual, spiritual, social and material. It's the individual's responsibility to fulfil these needs, but many people are either unaware of them or are unbalanced in their handling of them.

- **Physical needs** include food, rest, personal cleanliness, internal and external health, fresh air, exercise, sleep.
- **Emotional needs** include well-being, being at peace with oneself, healthy relationships, self-knowledge and personal development.
- **Intellectual needs** include mental stimulation, pursuit of interests, conversation, interesting work and/or hobbies.
- **Spiritual needs** can be met by the practice of religious beliefs or, in a wider context, through nature, creativity, children, animals, art, music, poetry and even sexuality.
- **Sexual needs** are usually met by sexual activity, but the broader concept of sexuality takes in connection to the lifeforce and creative energy so can also be accessed through communion with others in a spiritual way, as well as with nature and art.
- **Financial and material needs** are furnished by the earning of income and balancing input with output and enjoying the resources our level of income affords, keeping in mind the needs of the future with some forward planning and saving if possible.

Healthy boundaries and setting limits

A lot more will be said about this subject in the context of specific relationship stress but, in terms of general stress management, it is very important to have clear boundaries on such matters as hours of work, doing for others, rest and leisure needs, priorities, attitudes regarding health and overall well-being. No one has the responsibility of these choices in your life but you and this is where self-regard and time management come in again. I will look more closely at the issue of workaholism later—this affects a lot of relationships negatively.

No matter how much you love your family, friends, job, home and so on, you must learn to love yourself first for, without your own strength and well-being, you can't do much for anyone else. This is a difficult area for a lot of people, particularly women, who are socialised from a young age to give till it hurts. With men, it's more to do with work ethics and society's expectations.

Giving yourself rewards

This is a more important act than you might first think. We all have difficult or tedious jobs to do as part of everyday life but your attitude to them will make all the difference as far as how, when and why they get done. If you develop a philosophy of joy with everything you do, soon your daily burdens will seem lighter. It's the old 'whistle while you work' idea. The work has to be done anyway: it's up to you to choose whether it's a miserable business or a pleasurable one, even such mundane tasks as washing or weeding.

Added to this should be a habit of self-praise, a natural

childhood occupation but one that is given up in adult life for fear of appearing vain. If you've done a job well, no matter how ordinary, don't look about for someone to tell you 'Well done'—pat yourself on the back. This has two positive effects—you feel better about yourself and doing jobs in future, and you move out of the need mode so that any outside praise you then get is a bonus.

Rewards can also be something more tangible, for example, a rest period or doing something you love such as reading a book or going for a walk. I find I always work better if I promise myself a treat at the end of the task, like a child getting an icecream after a visit to the dentist.

Communication

This is a vital and effective tool for stress management. It involves self-esteem, confidence and assertiveness skills. Because stress has a cumulative effect, the buildup of which is often unseen, much of the tension can be prevented by clear, positive communication, some common examples being the establishment of ground rules in business and personal relationships, the ability to say no when necessary, asking for one's own needs to be met and rights to be respected, and speaking up in a helpful way when angry. Without these skills, pressure can build even in the healthiest relationships and can be extremely destructive in a struggling one.

I would go so far as to say that poor communication is probably the key reason for most relationship stress. It will be discussed in detail in chapter 2.

Formal techniques

If stress has already become a habit, you need to counterbalance it with activities that relax and relieve tension. The executive who plays golf once a week and squash a couple of days after work is doing a positive thing. It's very necessary to unwind after a pressured day at whatever work you do and sometimes exercise is better than rest.

Having pleasurable hobbies and interests adds joy and meaning to a life that can otherwise seem to be just one long grind. Pursuits such as yoga, meditation, T'ai chi, relaxation classes, and artistic interests such as pottery, craft, tapestry—anything that is soothing—are all excellent ways to combat the ravages of stress. Fun activities such as dancing, singing, walking, laughter and friends are all cheap and wonderful too.

Make life as easy as possible

Stress management does not have to be fancy or radical unless you have really overdone it, then, perhaps initially, some major strategies need to be implemented, but ongoing, simple measures are the best.

Do whatever it takes to change your life from a fraught, frantic existence to a smooth-flowing, calm experience. Think of a raging river and then, a silent stream. At times, you might have to be a raging river in life but when you are starting to feel exhausted from that momentum, picture the stream and you will actually mentally slow down. That is the beginning of your body slowing down, then your emotions, and so on until you feel the pace inside and outside you alter quite perceptibly. In the last chapter of this book, I will look specifically at some of these positive living strategies. For now, here is a small exercise you can use anytime you start feeling anxious or stressed.

Think about trying and conjure up in your mind's eye what 'trying' means to you. You'll probably come up with things such as effort, work, attempt, struggle, strain, stress, achievement. Now feel these words, feel 'trying'.

Next, think about letting go' Repeat the same procedure. You'll think of words such as freedom, surrender, release, peace, liberation, calm, ease, joy, comfort and so on. Feel the difference in your body when you do this second part. After a while, you'll start to feel emotionally lighter as well. I use this technique any time I'm battling with something that feel's difficult and straight away I feel better, different about it. I can put the problem into perspective because nothing at all is ever helped by worry or anxiety.

Before we leave this chapter, I want to dispel a few of the common myths about stress that are widely believed.

Stress is an invention of the twentieth century

Certainly, we talk about stress far more today than in previous centuries but as stress is a human condition it has been with us since time began. I'm often asked if I think stress was more prevalent in the 1990s than in any previous time and I usually say that it's not so much a matter of degree as a matter of complexity. Life is more complex today so most of us are living with higher levels of stress, even those who choose to live a simpler lifestyle. Stress is all around us so it's personal management that makes the main difference to an individual's handling of it.

Stress affects only nervy, highly-strung people

Temperament is a factor in the creation of and dealing with stress. Whether you are an introvert or extrovert will have a lot to do with your response to daily stresses. It stands to reason that if you are by nature a worrier, nervous or anxious, if you a perfectionist or a 'control freak' you will tend to become more easily stressed. That's why looking at one's behaviours is an essential part of overall stress management. Some people internalise its effects, which only show up when the person has burnt out as a result of overload. Others explode more easily when feeling stressed.

Neither burnout nor exploding are good ways to handle stress for introverts or for extroverts; positively dealing with anger and disagreements diverts the negative properties of stress. Every strategy mentioned so far can help to build awareness of the warning signs, from the small signals to the major ones. If left too long, major problems can erupt without warning.

Stress is overexaggerated

The ravages of prolonged stress are very real and scientifically proven, particularly the link between stress and disease. Stress reduces the efficiency of the immune system so it stands to reason that a stressed person is much more susceptible to viruses, infection and illness in general. It's the only rational explanation I can find to explain how some people who smoke all their lives can live to ninety while others contract AIDS after one sexual encounter with a carrier. Stress is the significant factor that makes the difference.

We saw earlier in the chapter how stress takes away enjoyment of life, reduces energy levels and efficiency at work, creates irritability and contributes to breakdown of relationships. Ill health is perhaps the most serious consequence of long-term stress but the short-term effects are pretty destructive as well and the sad thing is that most of it is preventable through education, positive choices and self-love.

Stress is always bad

A certain level of stress is not only good, but we actually also need it. Stress is adrenaline and energy and excitement and motivation —all good things we want and need, but we don't want too much and we want only to use them in a positive way.

We can harness the positive energy created by stress to use for ourselves. We must always stay in charge of our stress; otherwise it will control us. Athletes and performers who have learnt the art of managing stage fright and anxiety are doing precisely what I've described. They have grabbed hold of stress and turned it around for their own benefit. We can all do the same. Without stress, we'd be positively amoebic! (There's such a state as being understressed too.) So it's the amount that we need to monitor. No matter what our natural reaction to stress might be, we can choose to change and improve the negative responses.

Stress is the same as tension

I prefer to call outside pressure stress and internal pressure tension. That keeps it separate and clear for the purposes of discussion. Tension is what we feel on the inside as a result of stress; its degree will vary from person to person.

> **These are the specific points of tension in the body**
>
> the head
> the back of the neck
> the throat
> the chest
> the stomach
> the lower back

Depending on the individual, the tension within and the stress around you will affect a particular part of your body. Don't accept chronic pain without a physical reason—examine the possibility of emotional stress being the cause. The body is a reliable source of information about psychological problems. Some people are naturally more tense than others and they're more likely to be adversely affected by stress. An introvert will tend to internalise stress as it occurs, which is dangerous because the symptoms can then be masked. An extrovert will react with anger or yelling which releases the stress but erodes relationships and puts a strain on the angry individual.

It should be obvious to you now that stress can be very damaging—to health, wellbeing, lifestyle and relationships. We will pick up the theme of relationship stress specifically in the next chapter.

2. Relationship Stress

Having looked generally at the issues of modern-day stress, let's become more specific.

When there are two or more people involved in an interaction, it stands to reason that the potential for stress is intensified and complicated. Relationship stress is a special brand and can be ranked as one of the most severe sources, mainly because we're all in relationships in one way or another.

The suggestions for management in chapter 1 are applicable to this area of stress also, but there are special strategies that can help even further. It's easy to see that the less stressed you are personally, the less you will absorb from the people around you and, in turn, you will affect others less with your stress levels.

We all take out our stress, anger and frustration on others, particularly loved ones and strangers; loved ones because they'll take it and strangers because they don't matter in our lives. This is not a healthy way to unload our feelings, but more on that later.

Before we can deal with relationship stress, we need to own our own stress traps and habit (see chapter 1), so let's assume we've done that and are ready to improve our relationships.

First, I'm going to talk about general areas of relationship stress, in other words, stresses that affect all types of relationships—friendships, family, siblings, workmates, neighbours, strangers, every kind, then I will focus on personal relationships—marriage, sexual, living-together, permanent.

As we live in an interrelated society, our lives impact each other's, which means that we cannot operate in isolation no matter how hard we try. As the seventeenth century poet John Donne said, all those centuries ago, 'No man is an island'.

That is so much more true today even though cities and modern life have created a great deal of alienation. One could argue that you have a relationship with every single person who touches your life for even a moment or two, for instance, someone asking you the time or for directions in the street. How do you know what that person is feeling at that precise moment or the state of that person's life at present? Your response, whether rude or friendly, could make a big difference to that person's day. Okay, most casual encounters are just that, casual, and instantly forgotten, but imagine if your meeting with every single person every day had an effect on them. You might act quite differently.

On the whole, we are most polite with those who come somewhere in between, not close and not casual when, in fact, we should be nicer to those we love and at the very least, polite to strangers. Events such as road rage, punch-ups in bars and disagreements in shops would no longer be heard of if we were always polite and friendly. It might be worth evaluating our behaviours in this area because if you spend all day snarling or criticising or being anxious, think of all the stress you'd absorb every day. You'd then take it with you to work and back home at the end of the day.

It is impossible to separate the compartments of your life when it comes to stress. If you're stressed all day at work and have no outlets for that stress, you will bring it home, generate more, sleep poorly, and the whole cycle perpetuates. That's why awareness of the problem is so crucial.

> **Other causes of stress**
>
> So, putting aside personal stresses, bad stress habits and outside problems, relationship stress is also caused by
> - personal psychology
> - poor communication
> - lack of understanding and acceptance
> - past history
> - specific stress events
> - other related pressures
> - projection
> - poor health
> - provocative signals.

Personal psychology

One's past history, hangups, conditioning, belief system, insecurities—what we call our emotional baggage—impinge on all relationships, casual and close. With strangers, it can be in the form of taking an instant dislike to someone on first meeting.

> **This occurs for several different reasons**
>
> - the person reminds you of someone from your past who hurt you, maybe a babysitter or neighbour from childhood
> - the person reminds you of yourself but in a way that you find unpleasant, in other words, holding up a mirror that reflects a side of you that you haven't allowed or explored
> - the person is behaving in a way that you find offensive, rubs you up the wrong way or, as we say today, presses your buttons
> - it is a genuinely intuitive warning that this person is not right in some way.

Apart from the last one, all of these possibilities say more about you than the person you dislike because it reveals something of your own psychological makeup.

With people at the middle range of intimacy—acquaintances, workmates, casual friends—our relationship styles stem from what we know about communication, conversation, getting along, politeness, social skills, and so on. Your family background will have a lot to do with this, for example, if you came from a family where social skills were valued, or where strangers were distrusted, or a family who exchanged affection freely, these factors will all affect your behaviour in adult interactions, how you handle emotion and conflict, whether you're assertive, whether you're comfortable talking about personal subjects, whether you have good self-esteem.

Your nature too is an important factor, what your personality is like, what your position in the family was. Let's look at that for a moment because whether you're the first, second, third or only child in the family has a lot to do with the way you interact with others as an adult.

The first child
Tends to grow up strong, confident, capable, bossy, controlled, diligent, dutiful, responsible, a leader, and hard on themselves.

The second child
Is either rebellious and a little wild or sensitive, anxious, introverted and somewhat insecure.

The third child
Has the easiest ride as parents are older, more experienced, more tolerant; is often the 'baby' of the family and gets away with a bit more, is usually more indulged.

The only child
Similar to the first but is more self-possessed, self-motivating, likes to do solitary things and expects to cater for self emotionally, enjoys his or her own company, has difficulty with trusting.

It is in close personal relationships that our individual psychology and inherent problems will be most marked. As this will be covered extensively in later chapters, I will leave this for now.

Poor communication

As communication is a key stress-management tool, it therefore follows that poor communication skills in relationships creates a good deal of stress. I have never counselled a married couple with problems who could communicate well. Whatever else appears wrong with the marriage, the inability to sort it out in a healthy, clear and loving way is the main blockage to improvement.

Clear communication is necessary for good relationships at all levels. Stress is created when people have grievances they don't air, needs they don't express, problems they don't verbalise and wishes they don't articulate. It might be as simple as wanting to ask a workmate to stop a particular behaviour that you find very irritating. If you keep leaving it and leaving it, eventually it becomes an enormous pressure, whereas if you'd dealt with it at the beginning, it could be resolved quickly and simply.

That's just one common example. Think of all the ways that you could communicate better every day that would alleviate so much of your stress—being more honest, expressing yourself tactfully instead of critically, speaking your mind clearly, asking for what you need, saying no when you need to, asking for help. Communication skills, including the all-important assertiveness, will be dealt with in chapter 5.

Lack of understanding and acceptance

Acceptance is a vital ingredient in positive human relations yet from the time we are born, we are taught judgement—to deem certain things as good and others as bad. Acceptance doesn't mean that you agree with others totally; in fact, you may be completely at odds with their politics, ideas, lifestyle, behaviour and so on. But by accepting the person, you are in effect saying that you acknowledge differences without judgement. Making decisions about what's good or bad is okay as long as we take the subjectivity out of it. Then, it becomes evaluation instead of judgement. For instance, evaluating a child's homework as incorrect is good, but judging the child to be a bad student is not. The more acceptance we can foster in our lives, the less stress we will engender and the more we will get along with others.

Understanding takes a bit more commitment and most of us reserve this for closer relationships. Besides, let's face it, it's pretty difficult to understand another person even when we're strongly motivated. It takes care, love, patience and buckets of tolerance to build up a clear picture of what motivates, pleases, hurts, angers and so on, another person. It can take a lifetime and often, just when you think you're there, you discover a new facet or aspect you hadn't been aware of. Understanding engages the mind; acceptance requires only the heart. If you can't offer the first then try for the second. I so often hear people say, 'I just don't get that person—why do they have to behave that way?'

The answer may have to be 'I don't know'. Acceptance adds, 'But I don't need to know. They're not me and they have a right to do things that way. I don't have to agree with or like it but I accept them.' Think of all the parent–child conflicts this attitude would save because our children are not us no matter how much we want them to be; they will want to try things their own way. Evaluate and help, accept if you can't and don't judge. If you think this is hard, you're right, it is, but highly possible and very rewarding in the long term.

There's a saying that 'If two people in a relationship are exactly the same, one of them is redundant'. What is there to learn from someone who is just like ourselves? Very little. Perhaps this kind of relationship is closer to narcissism than to love.

Past history

Our past history has a lot to do with our choices in relationships, as we will see in the section 'Attraction and vibrations' below. What your childhood was like, whether you were close to your parents, your relationship with your siblings, where you lived and went to school, your growing-up experiences, early friendships, first relationships, breakups (if any), work choices, and so on are all relevant when it comes to the people you surround yourself with.

It's said that you can choose your friends but not your family. That's true but, as an adult, you still have the choice of whether to stay close to family members, see your parents, keep contact with your childhood roots. To a large extent, these choices form your sense of personal identity. Your external identity comes from all the physical facts about your life, your data. Your true identity runs a lot deeper than that. This book affords you the opportunity to look at a lot more aspects of yourself and have a fuller picture than you already do. If you don't understand yourself, there's no hope of understanding others.

I used to think that our past history had to be scoured for information that we then added to our bank of self-knowledge which in turn promoted personal growth. Now, my belief is that we have to unlearn the conditioning, negative lessons and painful experiences of the past in order to move forward unencumbered, thus bringing a whole, healed person to every relationship we enter. It's a tall order and one that we might spend our whole lives trying to accomplish but I think it's a worthwhile pursuit. Can we ever be totally healed of the past? Probably not, but the aim is not to forget or reject it but, rather resolve, heal and learn from it, to get comfortable with our past.

Specific stress events

There's a standard list of ten or so items such as moving house, getting sick and losing a job, that most of us would readily recognise as being stressful occurrences in our lives. They're not all negative experiences by any means as getting married and winning the lottery are on the list too. The common denominator seems to be change that we human beings generally find stressful. Anything that constitutes a life change, whether negative or positive, gets the adrenaline pumping and heart-rate racing. In relationships, it's possible to plan for these to a certain extent in order to lessen the stress, for instance, if there's a wedding coming up in the family, it's better to accommodate this by not taking on too much else, getting plenty of rest and cooperating with each other.

As I said in chapter 1, it's the chronic stress that is most destructive because we don't always feel the negative effects until we're seriously in overload; as well, stress is very addictive and can easily get us into entrenched habits that are then far harder to break.

Stress events that we can't anticipate are a different matter, for example, if a family member is suddenly retrenched at work, it will affect the whole family adversely unless everyone communicates, pulls together and supports each other—and that's the difficult part. Some people automatically retreat when hurt or frightened: we all deal with stress according to our own temperament. That's where acceptance comes in again. It's important to support without judging, criticising or forcing opinions—allowing the stressed person space and just being quietly available is the best strategy.

Other related pressures

Such pressures as depression, anxiety, financial problems, work stress, insecurity or fear will impact very strongly on a person's stress levels and affect their interactions with others. Feeling unable to cope personally does not help in reaching out to others.

Again, it's important to deal with these conditions personally and not expect healing through relations; otherwise, it's too easy to blame others for our problems and engage in such behaviours as projection which we'll be talking about next.

Depression

> **Factors controlling depression include**
>
> stress
> coping strategies
> self-image
> anxiety
> self-generated worry
> insecurity/self-doubt.
>
> **Symptoms include**
>
> irritability
> inability to relax
> inability to concentrate
> frequent crying
> dependence
> withdrawal
> inertia/lethargy
> insomnia
> self-pity.

Depression can be habit-forming if allowed to grow unhindered. I am not, of course, speaking of clinical or chronic depression, which are mental disorders and usually require drug therapy. In the normal course of our lives, we can all experience blue periods or wake up feeling down for no particular or apparent reason. The best way to deal with this is to allow it to happen—don't judge it or criticise yourself. Accept that you're depressed, get on with whatever you can and let the feelings subside of their own accord. In this way, the depression doesn't get a hold on you; it has no power once you accept it.

> **Strategies for handling depression include**
> - taking some action, even something small
> - creating a breathing space for yourself
> - willingness to change
> - building some faith in yourself and doing some positive thinking
> - physical fitness
> - improving your attitude
> - sharing your problem
> - letting go.

It's easy to see how depression can affect relationships: it's very difficult for anyone to penetrate the gloom of a depressed person. There's no value in saying, 'Snap out of it', as inertia is part of depression, rendering the sufferer immobilised. The only way to help is to be supportive without judgement.

Anxiety is worry about imaginary problems That doesn't mean the anxiety is not real to the anxious person; it's extremely real, but not based in fact. For example, people who suffer from obsessive-compulsive disorder are anxious about disease and germs, thus the need to clean doorknobs, floors and other household parts continually. It doesn't matter how clean these items are, the sufferer believes they are not; hence the compulsive behaviour. Eating disorders have a similar root in that the sufferer believes herself to be fat and therefore, no matter how thin she actually is, sees a fat person when she looks at herself in the mirror. There is terrible anxiety over body size and appearance in these cases.

Anxiety is not always based upon a physical fact, event or behaviour but often exists only in the mind. Many sufferers report that they feel anxious at the beginning and end of the day. This stems from childhood associations, for example, the anxiety felt on waking can relate to problems at school or a tense home life giving rise to these feelings. At the other end of the day, it's often fear of nightmares or bed-wetting, arguing parents or a bullying sibling, or the next day's concerns.

These fears can come back to haunt us as adults if we haven't resolved them. Anxiety can be experienced as panic and, in extreme cases, can lead to conditions such as agoraphobia which, strictly speaking, is a phobia about open spaces but in common usage describes a condition in which the sufferer has a fear of going out of doors, experiencing terrifying panic at any attempt to do so. Too much stress can also lead to panic attacks which feel like almost heart pain—gripping the chest and causing the pulse to race and the breath to quicken.

Being in states such as these is very frightening and causes a lot of stress, which impinges on relationships of all kinds.

Problems such as work stress, a difficult boss or colleagues, financial pressures and the like are what modern-day stress is mostly about. If we don't put these into perspective in our lives, we will allow them to encroach on our dealings with others. That's why relationship stress can serve as a clear gauge of other problems that we need to deal with.

Fear is a little different because it's more of an internal stress, what I prefer to call tension; it also runs a lot deeper and thus requires more work.

When we speak of fear in the psychological sense, we are speaking of the type that exists only in the mind. Two other words that start with the same letter come to mind—fantasy and future. Fear is fantasy because, as with anxiety, it's not real. The more we enable it to exist, the more it grows and the more powerful it becomes.

Fear is also about the future because it's actually impossible to feel psychological fear about the present moment; it's always what is going to happen in the future that frightens us. It's what I call the 'What if' factor. In our minds we build up fearful scenarios that seem so real we believe them and act upon them. We forget that the opposite is equally possible, that is, that our fantasy of 'What if' could have a pleasant result just as easily.

If, when we think of the past, we feel mostly sadness and regret, and the future makes us fearful, then, it's best to stay in the present and deal only with each day while learning from the past and planning for the future.

Fear is very crippling and sets up limitations in our lives that prevent us from living fully. It's caused by many factors, the most significant of which is insecurity. Insecurity is the main reason that we have doubts, suspicions and jealousy in relationships, all of which create stress and can contribute to relationship breakdown. Fear affects relationships very directly as we will see in later chapters. Insecurity also causes projection, which is the next point for discussion.

Projection

This occurs when we 'project' onto others some aspect of ourselves, accusing another of a fault that we're in denial over, some characteristic we're unaware of in ourselves or we refuse to see. It usually comes out of self-delusion or simply a lack of self-knowledge. Hitler was purported to have called Churchill 'that madman running across Europe', a clear case of projection. Another type happens when we project onto others what is rightly our own emotional baggage such as insecurities, hangups, childhood issues and so on. The only way to stop projection is to own these and commit to self-healing without dumping anger, attributing blame or asking others to be responsible for us.

Poor health

Obviously, poor physical health affects stress levels and relationships, especially if it becomes chronic. Good health is another issue of personal responsibility. Too many people give all their power of choice and decision to doctors and other health professionals when they could attain a desired level of fitness by taking care of diet, exercise, stress management, good sleep, work balance and self-nurturing, in other words, a programme of sickness and disease prevention and promotion of a healthy lifestyle.

It's no good neglecting yourself and then running to the doctor to get 'fixed' once your health is in an appalling state. Medical intervention should be seen as a positive strategy only when necessary. Your general practitioner or counsellor won't have all the answers to all your emotional, psychological and personal needs, so take responsibility for yourself and consult a doctor only when the problem is medical and you need drugs or surgery.

Health is a more emotional matter than most of us realise. The link between stress and disease is now well documented; it has been firmly established that stress reduces the efficiency of the human immune system. If stress if levels are allowed to run very high and remain unchecked over long periods of time (see chapter 1) they become destructive. Moreover, emotional pain can lodge in the body causing physical discomfort and chronic ailments, for example, tension headaches. Sometimes, too, being ill can be associated with such issues as the need to have rest, the need to be pampered, being loved and other associations.

I can testify to this from first-hand experience. For years, I had a mind set about being a sick person. I wore this label and continually lived it until I realised what I was doing and made a conscious decision to stop. I have not had more than an occasional cough or cold since—and that was fifteen years ago. When I was sick, I also allowed myself to stop working, which I couldn't do otherwise. I also remembered childhood nurturing from my mother, which was only given when I was sick.

Once I realised where my chronic ill health stemmed from, I changed not only my thinking but also my behaviour. For instance, I stopped working to the point of collapse; I now take rest as I need it, thus pacing myself better, I stopped living with undue stress levels and I practise prevention by not overdoing, by caring for myself all year round and taking vitamins and other natural treatments so that I'm not susceptible to germs, infections and viruses.

Health, like so many things, is an attitude of mind. Saying positive affirmations, such as 'I'm a healthy and positive person', helps a lot. Simple but effective.

Provocative signals

Stress in relationships can be caused by the signals or vibrations we give out to others. It is a key stress indicator in relationships and will be covered in detail later.

Having examined common causes of relationship stress in general, I will turn now to specifically the key issues in marriage.

Stress in marriage—key issues

- cultural, political and religious differences
- sexuality
- money
- boredom/staleness
- children/parenting
- communication
- alcohol and other addictions (see chapter 4)
- family/friends
- guilt
- infidelity
- immaturity/lack of self-knowledge
- power struggles
- defensiveness.

Cultural, political and religious differences

It might seem trivial to break up a marriage or even fight over these issues but if one or both partners feel very strongly about any of them, it can quickly create tension and build up to a problem.

Cultural differences might involve racial issues, the sort of food partners like, family background, styles of relating, social behaviour and such like. There's no reason why people from different cultures and backgrounds shouldn't be able to establish a harmonious relationship but it is generally accepted that marriages of this type are more challenging and require greater levels of tolerance.

Political differences should be kept out of personal relationships and not even discussed unless absolutely necessary. Unfortunately, if you marry someone who is passionate about politics or very one-eyed about the party they follow, it's hard to remain neutral or to keep it out of your relationship. Either you have to go in with your eyes open or agree to disagree, but arguing about politics is pointless, like fighting over which football team to barrack for. To each his own, I say.

Religious differences are a bit more serious because they involve matters of religious practice, spirituality, bringing up children, moral codes and so on. It isn't always possible to separate religion from personal life. For example, a few years ago, my sister was dating someone who went to church several times a week and twice on Sundays. It was always difficult making social arrangements with them and, while I respected the person's commitment, I admit to having found it frustrating on an ongoing basis. If it's possible to get annoyed on such a small issue, imagine if you were married to someone whose religion involved practices that you were unaccustomed to or that took up all their time. It's often hard to be tolerant when we're directly inconvenienced.

Boredom/staleness
Even the best relationships become stale after the initial flush of excitement. In chapter 4 we will be looking at the laws of attraction and the various stages of an new relationship, but for now, let me just say that it is pretty immature to expect a marriage or similar relationship to stay continually amusing and entertaining. There will be dull patches and times of disagreement when it almost seems as if the effort is weighing heavily on you and you'd rather be alone. It's the very nature of being with another person day in and day out that includes the mundane, even the tedious.

There are ways to keep recreating the magic and romance—but more of that later.

It comes back to not being codependent, not expecting another to make you feel good about your life. No one else is alive to cater to your sense of wellbeing—that is a personal choice and a personal responsibility. So, if you're bored, do something about it yourself—learn a new skill, take up a craft, hobby or sport, develop your own interests, make your own friends, be your own person. They say that bored people are boring people. If you live your life fully, you haven't got time to be bored and, most importantly, foster an attitude of joy about everything you do each day. A relationship is like a garden that needs tending and nurturing: it is separate from the individuals involved. If you neglect the health of your relationship, it can die, just as a garden can die. Water your garden every day by doing your bit to keep the relationship not only alive but also thriving.

If the relationship itself is stale, jazz up your sex life, go out together a bit more, talk about it and, above all, keep your sense of humour. When you're happy in yourself, it's very infectious and usually spreads to your partner. If it doesn't, that's no reason for you to be glum as well. Stay happy yourself and try not to support the other person in their unhappiness. Instead, set a bright example and remember not to feel responsible. Either your partner needs to do some personal growth of their own or they're just in a bad patch and they'll appreciate your standing strong beside them If you are in a relationship where your partner wants you to feel bad with them, rethink this partnership.

Children/parenting

Many marriages break up over parenting issues. The main problem is not keeping a united front and working as a team. It's tough enough being a parent but if two people are working at odds against each other, it creates a lot of tension in the home and the kids learn very quickly how to make use of these differences to their advantage. Children may seem to be the natural consequence of love and marriage but they should still be chosen and wanted. Parenting is a serious commitment and requires discipline, thoughtfulness, intelligence and consistency as well as love. As most of our hangups and problems develop in childhood, it places a heavy responsibility on parents to at least minimise the negative legacy their offspring inherit. Because parents are imperfect, none of us has a perfect childhood (whatever that is), but with all the information and education about parenting available these days, it's a little easier for families than it once was and there's no excuse for continuing to claim ignorance with regard to parenting matters.

I must mention step-parenting here as it can be one of the most stressful family situations. If natural parents experience difficulty with communication, discipline, fairness, honesty and all the other issues that challenge them, how much more so is it evident with step-parents, who are often resented from the outset and have to continually prove themselves? If they try to befriend the children, they're often taken advantage of and seen as pushovers. If they take a firm line, they are accused of trying to replace the biological parent, whether that parent has died or moved out of the family unit. A very fine line has to be walked between love and firmness in order to achieve the right tone. The same parenting skills are required but step-parents have an extra burden to overcome. I recommend that anyone entering this type of family situation would be wise to seek help from any of the organisations in their own state or territory that offers courses for step-parenting, for example, the YMCA.

Adoption is a little different, especially if the child is brought into the home as a baby or toddler. Here, the parents' skills will apply as they would to their biological child. In fact, an adopted child often has more safeguards built into the relationship because of government or agency checks.

To sum up, if you are part of a parenting couple, then you shouldn't go it alone, rather, work as a team and when you disagree, do it away from the children, sort out a compromise and present it as a *fait accompli*. Children need and secretly want discipline and boundaries. If you're fighting over them, it makes them feel very insecure and it will teach them to use manipulation to get what they want from you.

Playing off one parent against the other is common occurrence among children and in the case of divorced or separated couples, this can become a favourite pastime with the aid of guilt and resentment felt by the parent left with primary responsibility for the children.

The best rules for good parenting are to be yourself, be fair, draw limits and stick to them, communicate and, above all, love unconditionally.

Family/friends

Many people fall out over family issues and choice of friends. Since the dawn of time, hating in-laws has been a popular family pastime; poor mothers-in-law have earned dreadful reputations for themselves. I don't see why mothers-in-law are any different to mothers themselves. There are nice ones and not-so-nice ones. My rule is if you can't like your partner's parents or other family members and friends, accept them, be tolerant and respectful anyway. The problems start when we continually criticise people that our partners love, forcing them to defend these people and maybe even to choose between them and us. That's pretty unfair. I would never give up a friend I valued for a partner, but a lot of tension is created by constant fights over these issues.

A compromise has to be found, such as letting partners see

specific friends or family separately from you. After all, we shouldn't be expected to like or put up with people we don't enjoy but, then, we shouldn't stop our partners from seeing them. Even former partners, who can become a very sore bone of contention, have to be tolerated, especially where there are children involved. Sometimes, the ex is merely endured in these situations, while in other cases they have become valued friends. That friendship can create jealousy in insecure partners. Isn't it matter of trust? We can always find reasons to be jealous if we look for them but trust is a vital ingredient of healthy relationships and should be nurtured at all times.

It's particularly difficult when we can see that a certain person is harmful to our partner. All we can do is point this out and then let them get on with it. I had to go through a very painful episode with a friend a few years ago who was in a very destructive relationship. It was clearly going to end badly—as it did after two years—and I tried to advise my friend repeatedly to give up the person in question, to no avail. After it was all over, I couldn't resist the 'I told you so' comment and was told by my friend that she herself knew she was heading for disaster but had to go through the experience anyway. That whole episode taught me a very difficult but valuable lesson—that we can only care about and support our loved ones, never live their lives for them or make their choices or even influence them.

Another example was in an early relationship of mine where my partner's best friend was very jealous and manipulative. I actually liked him a lot but told my partner what I thought about his friend. I got told off, of course, and accused of hasty judgement and so on, so I said no more about it. Some months later, this friend tried to break up another couple then bragged to my partner about it. He saw for himself what I had sensed but his love for his friend had blinded his objectivity. Rightly, he told me about it but continued to love his friend. However, he now had seen him in a new light of his own accord and was a bit more cautious with him.

We have to trust people to make their own assessment of situations and people. We can offer opinions by all means but a lot of relationship stress is created by power struggles in this area.

Guilt

The type of guilt I'm talking about here is not remorse, which is healthy and positive when appropriate in relationships. Psychological guilt is irrational and based on childhood shame. When brought into adult life, it creates feelings of unworthiness, insecurity and low self-esteem, all of which affect one's role in a relationship. Accepting culpability when you are wrong is good; taking the blame for everything that goes wrong is not. Guilt colours our thinking and distorts our sense of reality, thereby causing further complexities in relationships.

Infidelity

A lot of people would say that infidelity is unforgivable and is grounds for irretrievable breakdown of that relationship. It certainly is a very serious breach of trust but I believe that extramarital sex or, adultery, is not in itself the reason for the breakup if and when it occurs. There is usually already some underlying flaw in the relationship; no third party can really interfere with a healthy partnership. I have seen marriages greatly strengthened, even enhanced, after infidelity has occurred but only when both parties were willing to look honestly at the problems and resolve to start with a clean slate. That's a tall order as, once trust is broken, suspicions and jealousies hitherto not present begin to rear their ugly heads.

Infidelity can occur because one partner has a higher libido than the other, one is feeling neglected or one is sexually less interesting or experimental, but often, it's not even about sex at all. Couples drift apart for any number of reasons and an affair is sometimes just a reflection of that fact. If two people are both motivated enough to stay, it forces them to examine their relationship with a view to improving it. It's all too easy for the offending partner to become immobilised by guilt and unable to offer fidelity for the future, and for the offended partner to play the victim and lose trust completely. Of course it's very hurtful for the person whose spouse has strayed, but once pride is put aside, an honest look at the behaviour of both people can lead to a renewed understanding of the reasons infidelity happened in the first place. Naturally, if the woman or the man make a habit of having affairs then that's a whole other ball game and has to be considered differently.

Infidelity undoubtedly would be one of the major causes of marital stress, especially if it becomes a chronic problem, but if it happens once, is an aberration, it should not automatically cancel out all the positive aspects of the relationship.

Power struggles

This is a general cause of stress and can cover many areas of a relationship. It usually begins soon after the first flush of passion and romance dies off, generally within the first year. A couple can experience power struggles over personal issues, finance, parenting, family, domestic problems, even smaller decisions such as shopping, decorating and holidays. Instead of learning about life and relationships from our partners, we let the differences between us become points of conflict. All the things we liked and admired about our partners at the start become irritations and we become possessive and defensive about our ideas, ways of doing things and behaviours. Every remark is seen as a criticism and becomes the basis of dissent.

The best way to handle power struggles is through good communication skills, having healthy boundaries and learning effective conflict resolution, which topic will come up again in various parts of this book.

Relationships are by their very nature potentially stressful and it's only through understanding, self-knowledge, patience, honesty, communication, acceptance and, of course, love, that we can minimise the effects of the various stress traps of any relationship. It is also essential to know about what makes relationships tick, why we're in them and the people we have chosen to be in a relationship with. So, let's move on to those subjects now.

3. The Nature of Relationships

I'll start this chapter with an acknowledgement and a personal illustration of the issues. Much of what I know about these topics I learnt from my own life experience, others around me and two therapists/ teachers—Grayam Howells, who works here in Western Australia in an area called 'Harmonics', and Michael Rowland, who is a well-known Australian writer and personal development speaker.

I was going through a dark time in my own life when I came across these two gentlemen: I'm not exaggerating when I say that their work is life-changing. There's a saying, 'When the student is ready, the teacher will appear'. That's precisely what happened in my case. It was recommended that I consult Grayam, and I was taken along by a friend to one of Michael's lectures. Two other influences at that time also changed my life—a little book called The Game of Life by Florence Scovel Shinn, a counsellor in the 1930s, whose book teaches the need for total faith in life—a tall order indeed—and a series of lectures on codependence that had me squirming with the discomfort of recognition. These lectures were given by Jesse Green, a New York psychologist who now practises in Western Australia.

Previously, I had been a classic codependent in relationships, hungry for approval, handing over my power to others, trying to control everything, feeling helpless most of the time, untrusting and fearful. I was already working in the field of counselling and personal development and, of course, was able to help everyone else but unable to find my own peace and happiness, which appeared to elude me. It all came to a head when I had a short love affair which, on the surface, appeared to offer everything I had searched for all my life. When this relationship failed, I lost my confidence and felt that I could never trust again.

It took my sessions with Grayam to help me see that I was simply looking at it from the wrong perspective. I needed to change and then my life would change—which is, of course, exactly what I was saying to my clients. It's not so easy to see your own problems.

I did change and straight afterwards, I met a wonderful person I was sure came into my life because I had done all this work on myself. This too ended after a few short months and I couldn't understand it, especially as the circumstances were so similar. It's only after I went through the whole experience that I could see why I had brought an identical relationship into my life so soon after I changed. It was precisely so I could realise how much I had altered. Only when we go through something directly do we feel the profoundness of it. If I'd gone straight into a relationship that made me happy and was easy, I would've taken it for granted, perhaps even been a little bit smug—'Look what I managed to get for myself!'

We constantly set ourselves little tests and psychological tasks and learn as we shine through them and when we 'fail' dismally. When it feels as though we've been here before, I call it 'learning the lesson you already know', which is okay because each time we move forward a little bit more.

I'm now in a stable relationship that's in its fifth year. The first year was tough because of my scepticism and wariness and, above all, my anger, but the point is, we worked on the problems together, weathered the storms and stayed together. When it's true love, you'll always find a way back to each other. That isn't romanticising the situation but a promise of commitment. Before I leave this story I think it's important to add that I had never had short relationships before these two. The shortest one previously was five years. One of my students suggested I was now learning faster. What an insightful observation.

I offer my personal story as an illustration of the issues of this chapter but also because I want you to know me as a real person, not an 'expert' who is trying to tell you how to live your life. Sure I have the qualifications and experience to teach and counsel and write about life issues, but I've also made lots of mistakes and I've experienced everything I write about. I only recommend what has worked for me and my students, clients, listeners and readers.

Emotional history

How does the past influence us in relationships?

We've already seen that who we are cannot help but impinge on the way we relate, our stresses, conflicts and choices, but why does this happen?

People always think that psychologists love blaming parents and miserable childhoods for all of life's woes. As a counsellor, I look at the past with my clients for information. We cannot deny that our past influences us, shapes us and, to a large extent, controls our choices, relationships and the problems we experience. I don't know about you, but I am not prepared to operate in the dark, hurtling from one crisis to another, having ups and downs without ever knowing why or how to change. I want to keep developing more and more self-understanding and that doesn't come from only what we learn but also what we unlearn. Having a clear and strong personal identity is vital to psychological health and, subsequently, to healthy relationships.

Looking at our history is often the beginning of understanding. When we can do it without bitterness, blame, judgement or resentment then true healing can start. We use relationships for healing ourselves—that is a plain fact. When we accept this, we begin to see why we make the choices we make, particularly in the people we get involved with at a deep level. I don't suppose there's one person on the planet who doesn't come from a dysfunctional family, so there's nothing to be ashamed of. Most of us had average childhoods, a mixture of sad and happy; some had childhoods filled with cruelty and pain. Whichever it was for you, denial is far more dangerous than opening up to one's own truth as it cuts off all potential for growth. If denial only created ignorance, we could muddle through, but when dark memories and hurts are repressed, they often come out in far more negative ways than if we just acknowledged them in the first place. As a friend said after a lifetime of denial and then the inevitable crash, 'I shelved away so much rubbish, there was finally no more room.'

We carry our emotional baggage around for as long as we stay in denial. Awareness of this and the desire to change opens up the way to healing. The job won't be completely done even on our deathbeds; it's an ongoing process, but if we never start, we are cutting off so many experiences that we could have. Yes, some of them painful, but do you want a life of fullness and consciousness or one lived in fear and powerlessness? It's your choice but if you're reading this book, you've already made it. It takes a lot of courage to say, Yes, I want to know the whole unvarnished truth about myself, my family and my beliefs and I want to heal myself. It's no wonder many opt for denial and avoidance, but in my work, where I see only people who are interested in growing, their courage and commitment is always rewarded by insight, healing and enrichment of life experience.

So, if you're willing, let's do this together. Here goes.

Childhood patterning

When we are children, our parents or other authority figures are gods. We watch their every move, listen to their words, feel their responses, believe everything they tell us. It doesn't take long to have our illusions shattered—researchers say by age three, the job is done, our influences set in place, our core beliefs beginning to form and patterning on its way. That's a pretty scary statistic for parents, I'm sure, but armed with love and knowledge, you can do a terrific job without fear.

Even after we are faced with the dull thud of reality after the initial period of undiluted joy that characterises our early days on earth, we still need to believe that our parents are perfect. That explains why a child dealing with a violent, abusive or even incesting parent, takes the blame and shame onto itself. It's not—'What a horrible father/mother I have'; it's 'What a bad child I must be to be treated this way'. We learn early in the game that we have to work around our parents' moods, keep them happy and please them in order to gain the love and approval we seek—the beginnings of codependence. Other misleading beliefs, such as self-blame, perfectionism, unworthiness and guilt, are learnt too at this time.

As we grow up we form core beliefs about many things, not just our parents and ourselves. We develop basic ideas about home, love, relating, money, work, in fact, all the key things that make up our lives, so that by the time we go to school, we have already formed and absorbed a whole belief system which we then take into the outside world. Our main role models, usually mum and dad, are our first teachers. We model ourselves on their behaviours, feelings, ideas and attitudes. Sometimes, later in life, we have to spend years undoing these if we find that they're not right for us or in some cases, have been destructive and negative.

If you were brought up by a single parent or if your

significant others were not your parents but a gay couple, two aunties, a parent and a grandparent or any other combination, this is what you will regard as normal. If your father got drunk every Friday night and beat up your mother, you will think that's normal, horrible maybe, but normal. It is this internal image of normal that you will recreate as an adult. That's why a woman who experienced violence or addiction in childhood will often marry into the same situation. Why?, I hear you screaming. What sense does it make? It makes perfect, logical sense. It comes back to what I mentioned before—that we have to live out our lessons before we fully absorb them. Once we have absorbed the new growth, it is possible to stop bringing pain into our lives, to learn our lessons easily and effortlessly, but not at first. We need the message in our face before we can see it. The trouble is that the thing we fear most is the very thing we will create in our lives.

Let's take some actual examples of how these core beliefs work in practical terms.

Core beliefs

Self

The first and most important one is the beliefs we carry about ourselves that dictate our self-image and the unconscious signals we give out through our energy vibrations. A person who thinks at a deep level that she's not good enough or is a waste of space or stupid will project this self-belief onto everyone she meets. She might then wonder why people respond to her in these negative ways. It's because every person we meet reflects back to us what we give out.

Situations, events and circumstances do the same so that the reflections you see in your life every day—your home, car, job, relationships, finances, health—tell you where you're at. You can only look in a mirror and see yourself: it's the same with these reflections—you are only looking at yourself when you look at your old bomb of a car, empty bank account, failing marriage, poor health, rundown house and hated job. Even if only one of your key reflections looks unhealthy, you might be creating a blockage in that area by limitation or negative thinking.

Most of this book is essentially a manual on how to break free of these old habits and patterns so don't get too bogged down on every issue and sweat on how to fix it. Chapter 10 will address this area specifically but remember that you only have to deal with you and all external problems will fix themselves anyway. What you think of yourself at the unconscious level will affect everything you do, the work you choose, the relationships you have, and whether you're happy or unhappy.

Work

We tend to follow in our family's footsteps when it comes to choosing our future employment, particularly in the type of work we want to do. For instance, if one or both of our parents have professional jobs and/or came from professional backgrounds, we usually follow suit. Exceptions will occur in cases where intellectual capacity or levels of interest differ so widely that this becomes impossible. Also, if a child is pressured too much to follow a parental or family trend, the reverse influence can apply.

However, what is even more relevant is our attitude to work and factors such as work ethic, the meaning of and motivation for work; it is these that will develop our belief systems about work. If you saw your father come in at the end of every working day in your formative years, throw his workbag down and curse his place of employment, your belief about work will be that it's something hateful that has to be endured in order to make a living.

People hold widely differing views about work, ranging from joyful and creative to tedious and inevitable, like death and taxes. Some of us even get addicted to work and use it to bolster our self-esteem; some like the prestige of an 'important' job or the opportunity to make lots of money, while others work at things they love without thought of remuneration. So, perceptions of work aren't standard and universal ideas at all.

What you end up doing has as much to do with your idea about work as your talents, skills and qualifications. Perhaps you were expected to gain a university degree, perhaps your family needed you to get a job straight after school to bolster the household income, perhaps you didn't need to work at all when you left school—these are all different realities, but eventually, you get to choose for yourself. When clients complain to me that they have no choice when it comes to their job, I try to explain to them they're victims of a mind set, not a fixed reality. We always have choices about everything and sometimes, when a person faces unexpected unemployment, they have found themselves pursuing a talent or dream they wouldn't have otherwise, such as flying a plane or playing a musical instrument.

Your attitude to work will determine how high you climb, where you physically work, the money you earn, every factor of your employment, so take heed: if you're in a job you hate, you have somehow imagined yourself there. As quickly as possible, imagine yourself somewhere else. If you want a job that is enjoyable, that utilises your talents, that allows you creative input, that offers unlimited growth potential, pays well and is accessible to your home, you have firstly to believe that you deserve it and let go of all your previous ideas about work that may be holding you back.

Money

As a society, we have so many negative ideas about money. Everyone says they want it yet most people only ever earn enough to get by, create too many debts and find that wealth eludes them. Why? We can only have as much money as we think we are worth, literally. If you think poor, you will still feel insecure and needy with a million dollars in the bank. This is what we call 'poverty consciousness'. If you think rich, you will do so even if all you have in the world is a $10 note.

In Western societies, we are judged by our level of material attainment, yet so few really ever get free of financial difficulty. Again, we learn our ideas about money from the messages we absorbed as children from everything and everyone around us. Common sayings, such as, 'Money doesn't grow on trees', teach us that we should be frugal and hold onto what we have rather than trusting in our ability to earn or receive more. Money is a currency; it's meant to circulate. It comes in, it goes out. Beyond keeping a watchful eye on the balance between these two actions, we should never worry about money or fear its lack, for the very act of worrying keeps money from flowing freely to us.

So much relationship conflict is caused by financial disagreements when it's so unnecessary. There is nothing emotional about money yet we attribute all kinds of emotional attachments to it, make it about power and freedom and security and happiness, none of which can be gained by money. A billionaire who controls several companies, runs a large corporation and employs thousands would soon lose it all if he did not have managerial abilities, courage, intelligence and many other skills. Being able to make money is a consequence of ability not the other way round. Freud said that money can't make us happy because it's not a primal need. It's a conditioned idea that money is desirable and that we should hold onto it so we can feel safe. When people tell me they have savings for a rainy day, I suggest that they should perhaps save for a sunny day instead, for holidays and luxuries and gifts. Wouldn't that be better? Keeping an emergency fund ensures that you will create the unpleasant emergency to use up that money, such as a car repair or unexpected household expense.

No matter what your job, income or budget, you have the choice of viewing yourself as rich or poor. Just be clear that these energies are a two-way flow. Like a boomerang, your thoughts rebound as physical circumstances. If you're constantly broke, look to how you might free your thinking of the blockages that are keeping you in that state.

Health

Physical health cannot be separated from mental, emotional and spiritual health as we saw in chapter 1. Hypochondriacs imagine they're sick all the time because of basic underlying fears about disease, death and being unsafe. There's always a payoff for everything we do, even when it appears that we're hurting ourselves. In fact, sometimes, self-defeating behaviour is the very point.

In the days when I thought of myself as a sickly person, my body obligingly created illnesses for me to cope with. We call this 'self-fulfilling prophecy'. Looking back now, I realise that I thought of myself as sickly because when I was a child my mother gave me more attention when I was sick than at any other time. When I grew up and took over the management of my own life, I could only give myself rest and nurturing when I was physically ill. These attitudes nearly killed me until, in 1982, I finally decided I had to change my life. The first thing I had to do was rethink my lifestyle, greatly reduce my stress levels and build up a healthy self-love that allows me now to make my life as easy as possible.

If you want a healthy body, you have to first create this idea in your mind, and then accept the responsibility for getting one. It is not up to doctors, politicians or our partners to take care of us. Physical health comes from a positive mental attitude, self-love and a balanced lifestyle.

Life

Your life is the product of your thought patterns and belief systems. All the details of your life and, let's say, the five main reflections—relationships, health, money, job, home—are your indicators of what you think about yourself. They are your mirrors and, no matter how hard you try, you can never see anything but yourself in them. Your job is you, your health is you, your home and so on. When you're healthy, so will your reflections be. If all your mirrors show unhealthy pictures, you know you have one major blockage to clear out. If there's only one area of your life that's showing up as problematic, you just need to clear that.

'Life wasn't meant to be easy' is a commonly used expression. Who says? Is it written down in stone somewhere or is it a consciousness most of us have accepted without question? If you expect life to be a struggle, that's what you'll experience. I believe that life was meant to be simple and that we complicate it with our fears and doubts and insecurities. Perhaps you don't believe that you create your own reality. Perhaps you think life just happens to you and that you are, therefore, a victim of your past, background, circumstances, financial position, job, and so on to infinity. How then can you explain those who rise above their limitations and disadvantages? Why does a positive person in a wheelchair achieve far more than an able-bodied person with a negative attitude? What you make of your life is dependent only on how you think and feel about yourself.

Most of us come out of our childhoods feeling inadequate, unworthy and unlovable. Does that mean that all parents are cruel, cold and critical? Not at all. The reason is that most of us are given conditional rather than unconditional love. While parents may not actually stop loving their children when they're naughty, difficult or disobedient, the child feels it that way because of the withdrawal of approval. This is often said straight out with remarks such as, 'I've had enough of you today', or 'Get out of my sight till you can behave'. But it doesn't have to be stated; it can be implied and suggested and felt.

All children want their parents' love, attention and approval, even those who appear rebellious and careless. We work out early in our lives that in order to get these things, we have to please our parents. As I said before, this is where the roots of codependence begin to form, an unspoken bargain of exchanging power—in order to be loved, I must do this or that. We take this belief into our adult relationships, which is why codependence feels so natural and comfortable.

Labels

The labels of our life—some from childhood, some from the present and some self-imposed—are not only limiting, but they can also be very damaging. For example, if a girl is told as a child that she's plain, she's likely to believe this utterly and live out an adult life of an unattractive woman instead of making the most of the assets she does possess. Many eating disorders stem from this type of origin, creating women and, increasingly, men who diet or starve themselves to forever cancel out the 'fatso' or 'tubby' label. A common example is being called 'stupid' as a child. Many people emerge into adult life believing that they're not good enough because of put-downs, criticisms, humiliation, neglect and other forms of emotional abuse.

There are only two things we can do with our labels from childhood—live them or disprove them. Take the 'stupid' label—a person who wears this subconsciously will logically grow up to live a stupid life, that is, doing badly at school, failing, dropping out, leaving school unqualified, being unable to hold down a job or working in a series of occupations with no success, always short of money, poor relationships, a 'loser.'

If, on the other hand, the same person determines to break free of this label, they may drive themselves unmercifully to disprove it, studying too hard, achieving the highest grades, feeling constantly pressured, getting qualification after qualification, building empires, owning property, piling success on success in order to never again feel stupid. This type of emotional rebellion is just as bad as living the label because the motivation is still negative.

The only way to get rid of a label is to reject it because it no longer fits. All labels are undesirable as far as I'm concerned as they limit us, inhibit us, stereotype us and take away our individuality. Don't wear them, even the apparently flattering ones, and don't place any on yourself.

My childhood label was 'sensible', which simply meant that I did what I was told without making a fuss. I grew into a very sensible person and continued to be sensible through all the stresses, heartaches, let-downs, illnesses, breakups and so on that came my way until I woke up one day and said, No more! Now I'm living as unsensible a life as I can manage by developing more spontaneity and self-indulgent attitudes.

A woman in one of my workshops said her label was 'sweet, kind and caring' and she added, 'I'm so sick of being perceived in this way!' Sometimes, we all want to break out of our expected behaviours, do unpredictable and wonderfully surprising things. Even if you only free your mind, that will release your labels because you're breaking out of the restriction of a set behaviour. Think differently about yourself and feel the liberation.

Polarities

Labels also stifle our exploration of all our personality aspects, our polar feelings, traits, tendencies, impulses and behaviours. As soon as you accept a label about yourself, you are denying the opposite possibility so a tidy person can never be messy, a calm person angry, a loud person quiet and so on.

In fact, we are each a mass of polarities; it's just that we simply make choices as to which of our features we show others and when. Allow yourself to be all things. You can be loud and quiet, rude and polite, silly and sensible. Play with the parts of yourself you have not yet explored. If, for instance, you think you are shy, experiment with your flamboyant, wild side. You will find this very liberating and it will help you to stop judging and criticising yourself and others. When others irritate you, it's often because they are displaying some behaviour you have not accepted in yourself (see the section, 'Projection', chapter 2).

Psychological health involves accepting your negative and positive sides, even embracing and celebrating them. Some days, you will feel like giving rein to your benevolent, compassionate side, other days, you might feel mean and cold. Accept this and you will find you don't need to live your extremes anymore. You will no longer be afraid to truly be yourself because that means being as you are without restriction or disapproval. After all, disapproval from others is also a reflection of your own self-criticism.

Trying to fix your reflections will have a superficial effect and will usually only bring temporary relief. For a permanent change to take place, you need to root out the underlying cause of the difficulty and release it forever. Tracing back to where the belief was first gained is the best place to start.

How do we learn these core beliefs?

Our belief system forms around the people who are most significant in our childhood, the things we hear, see, experience and feel, what is done to us, what is not done to us, said to us and about us, and how people around us interact with each other and with us. We are all born naturally joyful but, sad to say, that natural joy is usually killed off in small children before the age of three. It can be destroyed over time or in one dramatic, transformative event. Innocence dies and the inner child is trapped inside the emerging adult.

All our lives we will seek the wholeness that was lost in this way and search for healing of childhood woundings until we realise that we carry the process within ourselves, that we are not lost, only mislaid. We can come back to ourselves as soon as we understand that we can. There might be a need for some release work to be done, some surrendering of old beliefs, but the first step is always recognition followed closely by acceptance of healing. As a counsellor, I know that I can only help those who willingly want to change.

The trap can be as ordinary as a flower or colour or as sinister as a coffin or grave. These images come through to us quite commonly in dreams, drawings, writings or doodles. One client said she always found herself doodling coffins and she never knew why. How could a coffin represent an inner child's emotional prison? Perhaps the child was forced to confront death or a dead person at an age when she wasn't ready. Another client said her image was a daffodil—perhaps as a child, she had been absorbed one day in studying this flower and was suddenly shocked out of her reverie by a loud sound or a reprimand. One of the most interesting examples I've heard is a sexual abuse victim who asked me if I would like to see her doodles after I had explained this process to her. I said yes and she drew a sample for me. 'What does it look like to you?' The picture clearly represented the folds of a vulva.

It's as if the internal child-self goes into hiding for safety—we can feel it's there but we don't let it guide us or be real for us any more and it holds all our hurt. If enough layers go on, the child is buried so deep that it takes a lot of work before it will emerge, before it feels safe enough to emerge. Nothing outside us can ever heal this part of us. Only one thing can—loving our own inner child.

The subconscious deals in imagery, takes everything literally and operates on a different level of humour. Therefore, all the information that's fed into the subconscious from external stimuli and conscious thought translates into belief and, subsequently, behaviour. If your belief system says you're unlovable, you will create a reality in which you are unloved.

I heard a good saying recently—'Life is a dance and you get to lead'. Another way of putting it is—you are constantly writing your own script as you go along. If you don't like the set or the costumes or the script, rewrite it! It is as simple as that. You only think you're unlovable because of a childhood imprint placed within you by having parents who didn't touch you or each other much, being called unflattering names or not having time and attention spent on you. Spend time with yourself, care for yourself, value and praise yourself and start noticing the difference in your life.

If you want to know what your core belief about love is, for example, look at your relationships, look at who you deal with on a daily basis, look into the mirrors all around you, study your relationship pattern. What does love look like to you? Is it happy, liberating and joyful or frightening,stifling and wounding? It's not difficult to trace back once you've established this basic premise.

Vibrations

Vibrations are the signals we give out to others. They are based on our subconscious pictures of ourselves and the beliefs we carry. Vibrations are energy and we have no direct control over them. It is only by changing our core beliefs and patterns that we can start to give out a new signal and see different reflections. Reflections are just like boomerangs—whatever we throw out comes back or, even more literally, it's like looking in a mirror. You are always looking at yourself, whether you look in a real mirror or a metaphorical one. Of course, the image can be distorted by our own viewing, as in the case of the skeletal girl seeing a fat person in her own reflection. Another relevant saying is, 'I do not see the world as it is but as I am'. Perception is everything.

So, if you are seeing unpleasant or undesirable reflections in your life, look to yourself, turn the mirror around. Reflections can be in any form—the people around you, your home, health, car, job, financial position, so-called luck, accidents, crises, loss of job, relationship breakdowns, the lot. That's the place to start if you want to find out what you think of yourself—look at all the details of your life. You've created them.

Have you created positive, joyful situations and relationships or not? If you seem to lurch from one problem to the next, are constantly struggling and finding life difficult, you've got your answer.

Having assessed this situation, trace back to where you think each negative vibration stems from. This might require some digging and soul searching. Release will take more work again but you'll start to develop awareness and once you begin to let go of control and fear and mistrust and all the other defence mechanisms that are holding you back, you will be tumbling over yourself with successes.

The best way to illustrate this process is to offer some concrete examples.

First, you can effect change simply by desire if desire is strong and clear. I had a small problem with a student who was becoming too personal, wanting me to meet her for coffee and so on. I was happy to go along with this for a while but when she became more insistent, I asked Grayam for advice. He said to do nothing and she would just drop out of my life without discussion, if that's what I really wanted. I was astounded and asked him again and he repeated his advice. That very day, I received a note from her cancelling a coffee date and I was never troubled by her again.

Our subconscious brings many things into our lives that we don't even realise we want or don't want until we get it. For instance, when clients tell me their partners have left them, I always suggest they search their hearts for any desire to leave that relationship that they might have nurtured. Thoughts have energy and, even if it's months or years later, they can come back in concrete form.

The same scenario occurred for me in reverse some months later. I was going through a very difficult relationship crisis and had been spending a tremendous amount of energy trying to prevent a breakup. I was emotionally and physically drained. I was complaining to Grayam about this one day and he suggested I 'drop the ball'. I could not understand how this would help but thought I would try it. I stopped phoning, writing, enquiring, leaving messages—everything—and turned my attention to other matters. For a few weeks, nothing changed and I was very disappointed but the penny finally dropped that in fact, my disappointment and impatience were preventing the very reflection I wanted. I was also coming from punishment, wanting the other person to suffer for their neglect. As I said earlier, to change our reflection, we have to change within. After this, I truly dropped the ball and, in due time, I got the reflection I wanted and more.

It's all about controlling and then learning to let go and allowing the process take its own course. I have to also mention that when you make a new resolution, determine a new path or commit to a new skill, as the first step to releasing the old problem, you will usually have to experience a surge of it.

I have a problem with incompetence, am totally

uncompromising about it. Having expressed this to Grayam in one of our sessions, I experienced not one but three examples of it the very next morning. In my subconscious, I was furious about the first one, annoyed at the second and laughed out loud when the third occurred at about lunchtime, by which time the message was loud and clear.

One of the clearest reflections came to me when I raced into a large shopping centre a few years ago. I was in a terrible hurry with four things to do in a few minutes. I raced from one to another and finally stopped at the bakery for a item usually kept on the counter. A woman with a twin pram was blocking the whole front of the counter. I strained to look around her, thinking to move on if they didn't have what I wanted. I received a dirty look for my trouble so I stood back to duly wait my turn. The woman began feeding her babies their bottles and the assistant was calling out for her to take her change so that she could continue serving. This went on for a few moments until, finally, I said, 'Excuse me, the girl wants to give you your change.' The woman wheeled around, snatched her change, flung me another filthy look and flounced past me, muttering, 'Some people are so impatient!'

In that whole huge shopping centre, I had collided with the one person who matched my energy—angry, impatient, aggressive. I had to smile and I slowed up immediately. All relationships are just basically energy exchange. Remember that even when you meet a stranger these energy exchanges are working so if you feel instant dislike, attraction, interest or even a very strong zing, that's what's happening.

Our lives go through an evolution of events and

developments, changing us, helping us to grow. If we allow the not-so-nice situations to cripple us, we will indeed be beaten by life's forces, but you can rise above even the most dreadful tragedies.

The decade of our twenties is a practical time, thirties psychological, forties spiritual and fifties liberating. After that, we get to reap the rewards of the years we've already lived: how they feel will depend on the quality of the preceding years. If you have been mean-spirited, tense and unforgiving, your face will probably be badly lined, reflecting your struggles, your back will be bent over with anger and frustration, your knees unbending like your mind and your health poor.

It's all a reflection, remember.

This chapter has been largely psychological and will require some ongoing thought and work. To sum up, then. Your childhood influences form your core beliefs which are the root of your vibrations that you send out subconsciously and continually. These in turn create the patterns that you live by, ruling your feelings, behaviours, choices and the responses you get from others. In order to change your negative vibrations to positive, start by identifying your relationship pattern and work back.

4. Relationship History

The laws of attraction

THE LAWS OF ATTRACTION ARE many and varied but there are some principles that are accepted as basic. For example, we tend to mirror the people we meet so if I'm smiling, I'll usually encounter another smiling face, if I appear to like you on meeting, you're much more likely to like me back and so on. Remember what we learnt about reflections in the previous chapter?—what you give out has to resonate back to you.

There's also the law of propinquity, which is about proximity and frequency of encounter; it shows, for example, that we tend to marry people in our own circle and vicinity and of our own background and culture. Statistically, despite the many exceptions to the rule, this is borne out.

On a deeper level, there are two governing principles that are particularly applicable to sexual attraction. One is that we tend to fall in love with one of our parents (for reasons that will be explained later), the other is that we are attracted to people who appear to have something we don't have, something we can learn from, keeping in mind that relationships are for healing as much as anything else. Hence the belief that opposites attract. They do, but perhaps not for the reasons we suspect. It's not as superficial as simply being about a loud person fancying an introvert, or a shy, insecure person automatically gravitating towards a strong, capable partner. We do not fall in love with a person's looks or personality. That's just the packaging, the bait if you will, to draw us in. There is an underlying, subconscious reason for the attraction, that is related to our belief system.

Recall what was said earlier about core beliefs. If, for instance, your internal picture of love is that it hurts you have to find someone who will fulfil that image. Your inner radar finds and draws in the appropriate person to fit the bill while you're busy enthusing over hair colour, body shape, eyes and smile. Only when you get involved at a deeper level do you discover that you've married your father or your mother or whoever it is who has hurt you and will again in a new guise. That's why it's essential to discover your relationship pattern in order for you to see who it is you're attracting or marrying over and over again.

In cases of multiple marriages, it's usually the same person but with different faces. It's what I call 'learning the lesson you already know', but each time, you learn a little more until you no longer need to repeat the same choice and end up with the same result. These patterns would hold in all relationships.

It's not always a bad thing that the lesson is going on, as some relationships only exist to teach us painful lessons. When they're over, we realise this and, if we're wise, we thank the person who hurt us and move on. Feeling bitter and hateful creates a lost opportunity for growth—to say nothing of too much unwanted stress.

Let's take the first example, falling in love with a parent figure, which is the psyche's way of healing a childhood relationship that was either hurtful, lacking, missing or in any other way unresolved. A childhood hurt can only be healed by reliving it, which explains why girls who grow up in families with a violent father tend to marry a wife-beater themselves, revisiting a particular behaviour pattern from their childhood, just as would marrying a father figure who was chronically unfaithful or a mother who was hooked on valium or other drugs.

Then there's temperament, such as an aloof mother or an undemonstrative father. A girl with a perpetually absent father may very well make a lifetime's habit of falling for married men who in turn are unavailable to her. A boy with an aloof mother may well develop a lifetime of falling for women who are emotionally cold and distant. A child who had a very critical parent will usually be attracted to a partner who will feed their low self-confidence. It's all related to labels and core beliefs (see chapter 3). We pull in people to manifest our beliefs for us.

You would think that living this way was the last thing we would want to do but it does explain why woman stay in violent relationships, enduring physical or emotional abuse—or both, sometimes for many years. People say, Why doesn't she leave? What's wrong with her?

Women in these relationships cannot leave until they have worked through the pain and humiliation of being beaten, put down, yelled at, attacked at every level, until they're strong enough to walk out for good. That's why so many leave and then go back, time and time again.

I had a client who came to me with a horror story of mental, physical and sexual abuse suffered at the hands of her husband over a period of twenty-three years. As I listened, I could feel panic rising as I fought back the tears mainly because of the calm, resigned way the woman spoke. When she left, I rang my sister who, at the time, was working for a sexual assault centre and she advised me to exercise intervention immediately and get that woman out of her violent marriage. I replied that I didn't work that way, that I needed a lot more information and would need to meet the husband to ascertain his side of the story.

My instinct was that this woman was indeed seeking a rescuer and if I or anyone else supplied this service, she would never find the strength within herself to take charge of her own life. Inevitably, she would drift into another similar relationship if 'saved' from this one. I had to trust my own judgement and worked with the woman on this basis over a number of weeks.

The Christmas break loomed and I was afraid to let time pass without contact so I offered my home phone number with direct instructions that she was to call me if the violence got worse, even though it had abated. I didn't hear anything and in due course, she came in for her next appointment.

As soon as she walked in, I knew she had changed. Apparently, her husband had resumed his attacks, including raping her when she refused sex. Instead of phoning me or asking anyone else for help, she found the courage from deep inside herself to tell him to back off. She told him that if he touched her again, she would not hesitate to call the police. He could see she meant it and he moved out because theirs had been a classically codependent relationship based on his need to be cruel and her acceptance of this behaviour. Once her needs changed subconsciously, she not only found the power to break the cycle of abuse, but she also found there was indeed nothing that they needed from each other.

While you're busy falling for the external features you find appealing in a new lover, your subconscious is locking into the deeper, darker elements that usually don't surface till you're already involved. That's why you should never be guided by your hormones in choosing a mate, unless it's just for a fun liaison.

There are distinct stages to falling in love and romantic illusion clouds most of the first few. Blind passion is part of the magic of falling in love: we want it, it's wonderful, but it cannot, by its very nature, last. If you base a lasting decision on the transient feelings of this early period, it's obvious that the risk of making a mistake is high. Making mistakes in relationships is sometimes necessary, especially when you're young. But whether you've been in one long relationship or several shorter ones, you come to a point in life when you want to be happy with your partner, when you want the satisfaction of being with and loving someone without having to continually compromise or fight or make sacrifices. That comes only with and from personal growth—when you're happy with yourself, you will attract loving and positive relationships of all kinds. That is one of our most reliable reflections.

It's also important that you never feel you have to settle for any available partner. Doing so is a sure sign of low self-esteem. When it comes to a life partner, you have the right to be choosy. Wait to get it all. That doesn't mean you look for perfection or hold on to unrealistic expectations, but you have a right to fall in love and be happy, and to insist that certain features be present in the partner you choose.

Sometimes, older clients ask me if it's okay to marry just for companionship rather than heart-stopping passion. Of course it is, but only if you still believe the relationship's satisfying and positive. If it's just for convenience, I can't see the point. I've always believed you're better off alone than with the wrong person. It's all about hope and not getting cynical, especially if you're young and you haven't met the right one yet, 'yet' being the operative word. Open yourself up to the love you want and it will come.

❦

Nowhere is the pattern of working through childhood relationships clearer than in the area of polarities. That's why, if we live by them, labels limit us. This is particularly relevant in the conducting of our adult relationships. How does it work?

Let's say that you have a black and white view of yourself and, in turn, of others. You see yourself as having certain characteristics—quiet, tidy, capable, kind, reliable, whatever. If you do not acknowledge and experience the other parts of yourself, the darker, less likable parts, you will probably find a partner to do it for you. This is where the opposites attract theory comes in again. Have you ever noticed how many couples display opposing characteristics?

The longer two people interact, the more entrenched these differing behaviours become. We're attracted to the very qualities that we have not allowed to flourish in ourselves—that is one of the crucial points of attraction. However, after we win the person over, the qualities we once found so desirable become points of a power struggle. It's no longer 'Wow, my spouse is so lovely and quiet', it's 'Why doesn't my spouse ever talk?' If your partner never talks, it's because you chose them for that very reason, and now you want them to change! Whatever your partner is doing that bugs you so much, you do less of the opposite and I guarantee you'll both move towards the middle—if you want your partner to talk more, you talk less.

Very few couples are perfectly balanced; they're usually a combination of extreme roles and this isn't healthy. As the years go by, this becomes more and more pronounced and causes one of the key power struggles in relationships.

Let's say a woman suffered sexual abuse as a child. You might expect that she will marry a kindly, sensitive man who will be gentle and not demanding of her. No. It's much more likely that she'll marry a man who will push her buttons, force her to confront her old demons and face up to her sexual self. In this way, she can release and heal.

In the matter of polarities, we use our partners to play out our opposite personalities then we get angry with them for it. If I'm non-assertive, I will pick someone to fight my battles for me; if I'm scared of my sexuality, I will find a sexually demanding partner; if I'm an angry person, I will pair up with a person who allows me to get angry. This only stops when we realise we're doing it and take personal responsibility for change.

The best technique for reducing the existence of these polarities is acceptance—of self and others. It's relatively easy when you understand that we're all essentially the same; we simply choose to display different parts of ourselves publicly, so some people feel safe being shy, others loud, others aggressive, still others the life of the party, and so on. When you accept all the parts of yourselves, you will stop criticising certain characteristics you don't like about yourself. It then follows that you'll stop judging others.

A good affirmation to help you achieve this is saying out loud or to yourself every time someone else's behaviour bugs you: 'Mary is manifesting the — part of me that I have not yet explored.' It may be the deceitful part if she lied, or the selfish part, or the cruel part. There can be no blame or judgement when you acknowledge the same trait in yourself. Love all that you are, embrace it, celebrate it. Inside every shy person is a flamboyant one wanting to come out, inside an extrovert is a quiet, pensive soul, a daring bold warrior waits within the nervous and self-conscious and a poet is poised to bloom inside the toughest exterior. Let your many components find their expression and enable the complete you come out to dance.

In the next chapter, we will examine our myriad emotions and how we can reach completeness of self by allowing a free, unrestricted flow of these emotions. It is only fear that stops us, and the desire for control—again.

When you meet someone and feel an instant reaction—good or bad—you are connecting with either a matching or an opposing vibration. A matching vibration means you're giving out the same energy. Think back over the previous examples offered. If a woman enters a room and feels drawn to a particular man with a matching vibration, he is giving out subconsciously that which matches her needs and beliefs. So, if her belief is that men are violent or sex maniacs or dull, she will pull in the type she expects without even knowing she's doing it. On the other hand, if she meets a man who is everything she doesn't expect, she's drawn by an opposing vibration. The saddest thing is that, usually, the matching vibrations create a codependent relationship that will last, while opposing vibrations create a relationship that will be exquisitely happy for a short time but will generally not last. The reason is that the second type of relationship does not fit the internal picture and after a while, starts to become very uncomfortable, a bit like wearing shoes that don't fit.

Only with acute awareness and a good deal of personal growth can this situation be changed. It's very hard to give up something that is so 'perfect' and it says a lot about the human psyche's need for struggle and disappointment that we would want to. I may not have been the instigator of the break-ups of my relationships, but I certainly felt the discomfort and can understand why people just opt out.

If your instant reaction is dislike, there are several possible reasons. It could be due to what I call a flashback emotion, in other words, some associative feeling from the past has triggered a negative reaction. It could be that the person you have reacted to reminds you of some aspect of yourself that you find unpalatable or haven't acknowledged, like looking in a mirror and not liking what you see. Conversely, you might encounter someone who is displaying a behaviour that's not at all like you—at least not a part you readily accept—and your response is a mixture of anger, irritation and envy.

All these reflections that you see around you every day are a very necessary part of self-knowledge. We are surrounded by information and messages that help us to grow, but we have to be open to them. If we go around with blinkers on and choose to stay in denial, rigid and unaware, we are simply delaying our own freedom and healing. The more we know and understand ourselves, the better our relationships will be.

Here is an identity checklist for you to work on. Place a tick in the column against those elements you feel apply to you.

Your intuitions	
Your own speech—very revealing of real thoughts and feelings	
What people say to you	
What people say about you	
Your reactions and behaviours in various situations	
Dreams, particularly recurring ones, which bring persistent stress from your subconscious	
Others' reactions to you	
Body language—your own and others'	
Tensions within your own body	

We all play multiple roles in our daily lives and these roles affect the relationships we engage in. As is true of our internal and external identities, we should never mistake the roles we play with who we are. If we hold our own truth, stay in our power and have healthy boundaries, our relationships will be healthier and far more pleasurable.

Codependence

We hear a lot about codependence. What exactly is it? As the word implies, it is a blending of two sets of needs. If your needs and my needs dovetail, we are in a codependent relationship. But, you ask, isn't that what's supposed to happen? Aren't people supposed to need each other? Love and share, yes. Need? No.

The short answer is no. Codependent relationships are only the norm because the idea of them feeds our romantic illusions and our society promotes them. Think of all the romantic songs and literature in modern times. Songs and books that contain the sentiment, 'I can't live without you' in one form or another, abound in our culture. We've bought the myth and unhappily continue having codependent relationships until we realise there's an alternative.

Codependence denies a separate existence for either party and it occurs in all types of relationships. Symptoms include needing constant approval from the other, taking on the other's moods, hang-ups, problems and insecurities, enabling the other to continue their addictive behaviours, only feeling complete and happy when the other is, feeling responsible for others' happiness, alternating between giving in to controlling, needing to be validated by another, giving away your power, and not setting healthy limits.

Codependent relationships usually last because they form a comfort zone in which, in most cases, we can play out our parents' marriages. We get to work through all our negative beliefs, exercise our polarities and nag and whinge into the bargain. Unhealthily familiar. It only stops when one or both parties change their needs and therefore, their behaviour.

I had to watch a friend go through a most destructive and painful relationship for three years. I begged her to give the person up, offering all the most damning evidence and irrefutable advice. She refused to listen and, at the end of the affair, went crashing down. All the emotional energy I had expended did not save her from hurt. It was my first painful lesson in detachment; now I would behave quite differently if placed in the same situation. I no longer try to dissuade anyone from a certain course, just offer my opinion and leave it at that. I still care, but I recognise that it's their journey and I can only be an observer.

The clearest illustration of codependence is the one involving an alcoholic and his partner in addiction, whoever it might be, but let's say for the purpose of this example, his wife. They have a codependent relationship because his need is to drink and play out his self-hatred and her need is to be the martyr, which requires that she keep suffering. So she has to support him in his addiction. He comes home drunk many nights of the week, but every Thursday night, he comes home so drunk that he is sick all over the loungeroom carpet. She cleans up after him, often phones his work the next day to cover up for his not going in, then abuses him for being a useless, drunken swine. He in turn is getting his need to be punished satisfied at the same time.

Sounds sick, doesn't it? But would it surprise you to know that most of us conduct these same interactions to different degrees and in different ways? That codependence is a form of addiction?

I was shocked when I first realised how codependent I was. My long-term relationships were based on this premise totally but when I stopped being codependent, each relationship lasted only another six months. The two people in question were simply not ready to accept cocreative relationships in which each partner was separate and complete, and together share time, space and love. This idea was too threatening to both these partners, who mistook my detachment for lack of commitment.

Addictions

Addiction is the longing for something outside ourselves that will make us feel fulfilled, powerful, complete (though, once reached, these feelings, in these circumstances, are very short-lived). We generally come to think of addictions such as the excessive use of alcohol, cigarettes, drugs or gambling as being the need for negative support. Even an attachment to something positive—love, work, religion, sex, food, money—if taken to an extreme level can become obsessive and, therefore, addictive.

All types of addiction, including codependece, are harmful to relationships and a major source of stress. While, they should not be viewed as a relationship issue, in a codependent relationship, all types of addictions become shared; often, they are the cement that holds the union together. When one party decides to break the codependence, that relationship has to either radically change or it will simply have to end.

Addiction is more about being an addictive personality than it is about the object of our addiction, our drug of choice. So, once again, we can only deal with change by owning our own behaviour and what our needs are.

No one else can ever stop our addictive cravings. Indeed, we ourselves cannot until we look at what the root of those needs is—are we trying to feed a childhood hunger, deal with self-hatred, drown out old hurts and pains, suppress rage or open up parts of ourselves we're too scared to face? All of these can be done without chemical substances, alcohol, pills, excessive food or self-abuse in any form. It takes courage though, and commitment to total honesty and trust.

If you have an addictive partner or child or parent, offer your love and support but don't get hooked into their paranoia or their need for you to play out their opposite role—don't be a martyr or a punisher or an enabler. Set boundaries (see below). If you are an addict yourself, don't blame anyone else for the situation you're in. Decide if you want to change, then, if you do, ask for help from the appropriate sources.

Self-sabotage

The saddest kind of addiction is that of self-defeating behaviour. This can take many forms, all of which lead to sabotage of everything that is good and distrust of anything that is positive, as well as to cynicism, fear and a life that is mostly struggle.

Fear of intimacy is a particular case that affects relationships directly. Fear of all kinds manifest itself as the need to control. Controlling makes us feel safer but it's a false security. Like a house of cards, it folds under the smallest amount of pressure.

Most people will freely admit that loving and being loved is the thing they want most, yet so few people are truly open to it. Romance, yes, but true spiritual communication and connection, no. The latter makes us feel too vulnerable, too at risk, brings out our fear of rejection, disappointment and hurt so it's safer to skim the surface or, better still, lock up our deeper feelings altogether. Too much self-protection can be crippling.

Boundaries

I've come to think of the setting of boundaries as the most significant tool in reducing relationship stress. Boundaries and detachment are about personal space, power and freedom. Setting boundaries allows positive exchange between two or more people without aggression, anger, loss of dignity or principle.

Detachment is simply a separation from emotional response; removing yourself from the centre of feeling about a problem or situation gives more clarity and insight. In counselling, I cannot help a client who is too stressed as this clouds their judgement and confuses the issues. Detachment is the first rule of anger management, problem solving and conflict resolution as well. It does not mean not caring but it does delineate an invisible line between you and others, allows space and ensures that you don't invest all your energy in dealing with other people's responsibilities. This division is known as a boundary.

There are three main types of boundary—physical, emotional and sexual. Here's an example of each.

A physical boundary delineates body space and is in your charge so that if you're not comfortable in a place, it's your responsibility to remove yourself from it, for example, at a party you're not enjoying or in a cramped space where you're being leaned on.

Emotional boundaries are particularly important in relationships where problems, insecurities and feelings can easily cross over. As we've seen, in codependent relations, two people seem to merge emotionally and stress over the same things. Sharing and concern are different to this. If you have a healthy emotional boundary operating, you do not take your partner's, friend's or family member's problems on board. You offer advice, support and love but draw the line where you feel it's appropriate.

Sexual boundaries
Sexual boundaries ensure that you never have to do anything in bed that you don't like or take responsibility for a partner's sexual pleasure.

Intimacy

Intimacy comes in many forms and doesn't have to be sexual. Be open to intimacy with your children, friends, animals and nature then you will never lack this important life component. Feel your own emotional energy and let it flow freely, without expectation or judgement. Every time you invest in a relationship and it sours or ends, you feel discouraged and vow to never risk again, but love always comes once more—different and always brand new. Every day, take a chance on love and all those other things that make us human, including failure and mistakes.

5.
Communication

I HAVE NEVER COUNSELLED OR worked in a class or seminar with a couple who had good communication. Whatever their problem ostensibly is, it is the fact that they can't communicate clearly and effectively that makes a couple feel hopeless in their relationship. Therefore, I have to draw the conclusion that communication is the single most important tool in having a positive relationship, no matter who with. So many misunderstandings, disputes, power struggles and so much stress could be avoided if people learnt to share thoughts and feelings honestly and fearlessly.

> **Some general pointers on improving communication skills**
>
> - Remember that communication is always a two-way process, even if one party is apparently inactive.
> - Develop good listening skills.
> - Ask, don't tell.
> - Say it once; don't repeat your point or nag continuously.

> - Speak only from the first person, that is, yourself.
> - Own your own feelings and express them honestly.
> - Keep anger out of it.
> - Stay in the current situation.
> - Strive for clarity in what you say and what you hear.
> - Don't argue if you disagree; state your truth and respect the other person's point of view.

These pointers also encapsulate the skills of effective conflict resolution. If a situation has become chronic, a formal approach to solving the disagreement may be needed. That's one of the roles of counselling or the mediation process, which is similar to the function of the arbitration court in industrial disputes. If two or more people want to sort out their differences without an independent observer or a mediator, there are some simple procedures that work well.

> - Release anger and aggression before sitting down to discuss the problem,
> - Each person takes a turn to outline his or her position.
> - Everyone reiterates and clarifies the issues raised before moving on.
> - Brainstorming for positive alternatives to behaviour and future initiatives.
> - A consensus is reached on a way to proceed that everyone agrees to try.
> - A date and time for review is set.

An important point to mention here is that the stated dispute may be disguising a larger problem. Let's say that in a workplace, a group of coworkers decide they need to sort out a dispute concerning hours, duties, and so on. This is fine, unless the real issue is a lack of job satisfaction. If no one is prepared to state this, then the true difficulty will not be exposed and only a superficial benefit will come from any efforts to resolve the conflict.

It's the same in the home. If a wife says she's fed up with her husband working late every night and she talks to him about the fact that she's got to keep meals hot and deal with the family on her own, the truth may in fact be that she's feeling unloved, neglected, alone. It's much easier to be angry about trivial things than to admit fears, vulnerability and hurt.

Thus, conflict resolution will only work when the real cards are on the table.

To prevent stress as far as possible, it's necessary to develop good communication habits that keep the lines clear between members of a family or a workplace or a marriage.

Ground rules have to be stated and understood. It's no good saying after the fact that someone else should have known—a common cry. We each must take responsibility for getting what we want and making ourselves heard. This is called assertiveness; difficult as it is, it's a most vital communication and relationship skill.

Assertiveness is the middle ground between passivity and aggression. Most of us are more passive when we're younger because we're anxious to be liked so we tend to go along with what others want. We're afraid to speak up or assert our rights for fear of disapproval and rejection. It takes maturity, self-love, confidence and healthy boundaries to create a foundation for assertiveness and even then, on some days, we can 'fail' miserably. In everyday situations, such as sending back a meal that's different from what we ordered or insisting on our place in a queue, we are forced to confront the issue of our rights. When we first begin to develop this skill, we are usually much more strident about it because it feels so awkward and scary. As the familiarity of asserting ourselves grows, it becomes more comfortable and we gradually find it easier and easier.

> **Follow these very simple rules**
> - Speak your truth quietly.
> - Say it once.
> - Don't stop to argue.
> - Come from love.
> - Hold your own power and allow others to keep theirs.

When we're passive and we don't stand up for ourselves, we let ourselves down; when we are aggressive, we take away another's rights and dignity. Neither is healthy nor satisfying.

Assertiveness is an excellent stress management tool because passivity creates a lot of unresolved, pent-up anger and aggression, which is extremely stressful on both the body and the psyche. That's why the work suggested at the beginning of the book is so vital. The more you do on yourself, the more you will naturally find your way to these skills that minimise stress and maximise positive relationships.

A very good way to minimise the negative risks of destructive relationships and making the wrong choices, especially in one-to-one personal relationships, is to sign a relationship contract. This can be made part of marriage/commitment vows or a separate exercise to ensure that two people or a group are on the same wavelength and prepared to commit to the same values. A lot of people find this idea unromantic but my answer to that is that divorce is far more unromantic. If you're having a love affair, suitability and compatibility are less relevant, but if you plan to make an official or long-term commitment to a relationship, it's essential that you know a bit more about a partner than their eye colour and favourite cake.

I'm often amazed at the casual attitude with which people enter marriages and even business partnerships. Clients have told me that after whirlwind romances they've woken up a few months later and found themselves living with and/or married to a totally unsuitable stranger.

At least the basic questions of raising children, financial responsibilities and personal values need to be addressed, surely? A lot of church groups offer premarriage counselling, which I'm very much in favour of, and also life-skills training, including such issues as relationships, communication, self-knowledge, emotion, parenting and the like. These skills should be widely taught in our schools. Knowledge is power, so there's not much point complaining about how much marriage and family breakdown costs our communities every year if the knowledge about how to best maintain these relationships is not being widely disseminated. We need to accept personal and social responsibility for positive change.

A relationship contract premarriage, or even at the outset of a personal liaison, forces the parties involved to look at the key issues in relating (and cohabiting, if relevant). If too many issues are in dispute and can't be resolved, there's a good chance the relationship won't work. This is the time when the decision can be made as to whether it's better to let it go or, if there is sufficient commitment, how the differences can be breached.

> **Some simple inclusions**
> - What you want from the relationship.
> - What you have to put in.
> - What is your long-term view of relationship.
> - Your attitudes on money, children, religion, family, homelife, friends, work and so on through all the key areas of your lives.
> - Agreement on future policy regarding honesty, communication and the like.
> - Your specific needs and desires.
> - Ground rules for key areas.

If you can't communicate before you move in together, marry or start a business together, you certainly won't afterwards.

Communication is especially important when it comes to parenting and family issues. Most problems with teenagers, for example, stem from the inability of one or both sides to bridge the generational and understanding gaps. It is vital that families communicate well and it starts with the parents. If two people are not united in parenting, children pick up very quickly on that divisiveness and often manipulate it to their own ends. This creates general dissension and tension in the home. Regular family conferences are a good strategy to combat these breakdowns in communication. Differences can be aired in an open forum and everyone is allowed input that empowers each family member rather than having a chief and Indians situation.

Your family background will, to a large extent, dictate your communication style (see chapters 3 and 4). Therefore, it will also affect your adult relationships. I remember seeing a man in his seventies being interviewed after he'd done a three-day workshop in which part of the therapy was to cry for a whole day. When he was interviewed, he was still crying; he said he couldn't stop because he'd come from a family where talking, laughing, crying and showing emotion of any kind was not allowed so he'd grown up unable to display his feelings. The liberation he felt at being able to cry freely unleashed all those years of pent-up, unexpressed emotions: now that it had started he couldn't turn it off.

We spoke earlier about walls and boundaries. If you can understand that your partner's or parent's or sibling's or friend's or workmate's wall is a defence mechanism because of an insecurity that most probably has little to do with you or a temporary need for space, you can stop yourself taking it personally and wait quietly until they choose to bring the barrier down. This also applies to moods. When you accept your right to have moods and connect with your dark side, you will be more tolerant of this in others.

We spoke of loneliness in the last chapter, but there's a feeling that can hurt far more and takes longer to work through—isolation. When you feel isolated, you feel cut off from everyone and everything. In a relationship, this can spell death because you lose connection, closeness, intimacy, everything that's important to keep a relationship on track. It can also create problems in family units, for example, if a father doesn't know how to communicate and isolates himself emotionally, the burden of parenting tends to fall onto the mother. It's also a key communication problem between teenagers and their parents. In a marriage, it creates tension, fights, protracted periods of silence.

Love

The $64 000 question—what is love? It's caring, concern for another, sharing, communication, understanding, kindness and all the good things, of course, but it's actually not about another person. Love is part of our lifeforce and therefore we carry it inside us at all times. No one can ever say they have no love in their life because inside you, you are full of love; you are made of love. It springs from you like the seeds of happiness we'll speak of later. You only have to desire it, feed it and let it out.

Love is the antithesis of fear. The two are complete opposites: where one exists, the other cannot. So, if your heart is full of fear, you are pushing out love and denying it in your life. Feel it in yourself then offer it to everyone without discrimination. After all, you can't ever run out. Just give it and let it flow back to you; it has a boomerang effect. This is not personal love but spiritual love.

Of course, if you're waiting to be loved in return or give your love conditionally, you are quite possibly going to be disappointed, for love often comes from unexpected sources. If you share love with the homeless or strangers on the street or people you work with, you might get love from your family or a pen friend or your local priest. It's always available. Even when no one appears to be loving you, you can always love yourself.

Giving

Love does not mean unending giving, which a lot of people think it does mean. Endless giving is sacrifice, struggle and martyrdom, not love at all. Always examine your motives in giving. Are you doing it for praise, because you really want to, because it gives you joy or because you think you have to? If you give and give until it hurts, you will deplete yourself, eventually fall into a heap and resent the very people you have given so much to. Did anyone say you had to give so much or is this the result of your own conditioning? Do you feel more worthwhile, do you think it would guarantee you love, do you give out of codependence? Of course it's wonderful to be a giver, but give out of abundance, not out of need. Give because you have so much yourself.

In order to keep up your own supply of energy and joy, give to yourself first then you will overflow and that overflow is what you can offer others—without pain or difficulty or resentment. It will be easy and because there's no cost, there's no price tag.

How do you 'feed' yourself? Try to fulfil all of your needs every day, not just your basic needs of food, drink, air, shelter and cleanliness; they just sustain life. Also care for your emotional needs by loving and supporting yourself—your psychological by following your dreams and living a full, interesting life, your spiritual by enjoying music, nature, art and your own creative inclinations.

Hold your own power and don't allow others to suck energy off you. They won't be able to if you maintain your boundaries, but most of us just hand over the reins and waste ourselves pleasing others all day until we become so tired and fed up that we end up hateful and bitter. If you have to count the cost of the love, friendship or the giving you offer, it's better not to do it at all, especially in regard to your children. They don't want to have to be held to ransom for the rest of their lives because you brought them into the world and then calculated in dollars and cents all the love you gave, or efforts and sacrifices you made. Be more selfish then you won't have to feel cheated because, at the end of your life, you'll know you pleased yourself, had a jolly good time and have no one but yourself to blame for any perceived failures or disappointments you encountered along the way. In short, your life belongs to you, twenty-four hours of it each day, to be used as you wish, and not to be squandered. It is too precious a gift to be unappreciated.

Life stages

In chapter two, I spoke of personal psychology as a factor in relationship stress. Another issue, which connects with that and affects communication, is stages of life. The generation gap, as we all know it to be called, speaks of the distance between people of different age groups. It usually refers to a chasm, but it could be a bridge.

Parents and their children have difficulties communicating because the age difference between them is usually a chasm. Values, ideas, sources of information, public perceptions all change—a thousand things are different from one generation to the next. Rigid opinions and intolerance will create distances that are unbreachable. I wrote a lot about this in Teenagers and Stress, which would be helpful to you if you are grappling with this issue in your family life.

With regard to marriage and similar relationships, there are various significant stages of development that affect individual psychology and emotional states. Men experience identity crisis at around twenty or twenty-one and again at around forty, the latter period being known as male menopause or mid-life crisis. Women's times are at twenty-five and the early thirties. At these periods of life, a person is put through intense changes—priorities shift and, at a very deep level, emotions are tested and fine-tuned. Nothing can be the same after this so, naturally, these changes affect relationships, especially the more personal ones.

Imagine a home in which there might be a teenager, a young man or woman, a father going through mid-life crisis and a woman experiencing menopause! This would be a hotbed of seething emotions, with no one able to compromise or give ground because of personal pressures.

These are times where communication becomes even more vital, so space as required can be requested, clear boundaries held and positive affirmation given, even to family members who are being difficult to live with. There will be clashes, but remember: it's not fighting that hurts or breaks people up, it's indifference, callousness and anger. Express your differences, air your grievances, insist on being heard and respect others' feelings. Healing can take a long time; you don't want to make yourself and everyone else miserable in the meantime.

❦

People often ask me what to do when rifts have already taken place. Most rifts can be easily mended but for one thing—false pride. If you think you've been wrong, apologise, if you don't, say so, but be willing to listen to the other's complaint. Come from love—real love is endlessly patient, though we humans are not.

I'm not suggesting that the only way to have healthy relationships is applying for sainthood; quite the contrary, in fact. It's better always to be honest about your own shortcomings and forgiving of others'. Forgiveness comes easily when you remember your own imperfection. When you love yourself, you no longer need to strive for perfection because love doesn't judge or criticise. You can just be yourself, with all that that means, and accept everyone on the same terms.

The longer a rift is allowed to sit unattended, the harder it is to fix. So often I hear from clients that when they have approached family members, for instance, who they've fallen out with, sure that they would be rejected, they have instead been met with open arms and an attitude of, 'I've been wanting to approach you or broach the subject for years. Thank you for coming forward.' Even if this doesn't happen and you are knocked back, you have still done the right thing, a generous thing, and you've tried.

The result is not the only victory. We all dread rejection and will do anything to avoid it, whether in the boardroom or the bedroom, but if we are true to ourselves and come from truth, integrity and love, we need have no fear of the opinions of others. Avoid pomposity or arrogance, because we can always learn from others; in fact, every person we meet is our teacher.

By the same token, to accept others' ideas without question is not empowering. Ask, listen, respect, learn, but be your own person. None of us likes to be criticised or attacked, but defensiveness shuts the door to learning and open exchange, which further our knowledge of ourselves and aids in positive interaction.

Communication is an art and a skill that you can practise along with all the other life skills and for every 'failure,' you will move forward a long way and you will find others willing, indeed, eager, to share with you one of the wonderful gifts and joys of human existence—the sharing of ideas and thoughts. Don't forget that a large percentage of all human communication is nonverbal—you can say as much with a smile, a touch or a hug as you can with words, sometimes more. When words fail you, let there be communication in your silence through warmth, caring, compassion and love. That will reach people just as well. Communication is not about talking or oratory; it's about sharing, and we can all do that.

Sex

Sex is a form of communication and a particularly important one in relationships. We tend to limit our lives by limiting our thinking and in our society, sex is generally thought of only as basically three things—genitals, intercourse, orgasm—in that order. Sex is a lot more than that. Between two people, it can heal, uplift, comfort, refresh, spiritually join, create love and, of course, make a baby. Yes, it can also cause rancour, power struggles, spite, conflict, frustration and isolation. But if we stop thinking of sex as being only about physical pleasure and satisfaction, it will expand into the mystical experience it have the potential to be.

It is said that sex only features greatly in a marriage when it isn't working and I basically agree with that. In its rightful place, it is only one element of a loving relationship, only one of many ways to be close and stay close.

Sexuality is part of the lifeforce. It is energy in the same way that the emotions, spirituality, creativity and joy are energy. There is no separation and no lack. It's always available.

So, whether you are having regular physical contact or not, you are always sexual and you are sexual twenty-four hours a day throughout your whole life. Therefore, it's illogical to feel guilty about sexual feelings, needs and desires. Sex begins in the soul, is ignited in the mind, then translated into physical action.

We are not machines or performing seals. Some days we feel

sexy, some days we don't. Some days we can orgasm and other times we don't feel like it. These behaviours shouldn't be quantified or qualified. The two biggest concerns about sex for most people are guilt and being good enough at it. Think of how liberating it would be if they were removed. Sex should be a natural, pleasurable activity, yet couples fight more about this issue than almost any other.

There is no such thing as normal sexual behaviour. What is right for one person is not necessarily the best for another and we shouldn't judge it. To some people, nothing is normal except the missionary position. Well, that's fine for them, but there's a lot more adventure, fun and experimentation to be had than that. What you do is only limited by the extent of the individual's imagination. In our society, there are so many myths surrounding sex, so we need to separate fact from fantasy. Trust your own instincts in this as in everything else.

> **Main causes of sexual stress in relationships**
> - one partner wanting more sex than the other
> - sexual dysfunction
> - hangups and inhibitions
> - one partner using sex for bargaining, power or blackmail
> - sexual addiction in one or both.

If one partner wants more sex than the other, the only answer is to compromise. It's difficult in this day and age to make love daily, but two to three times a week is acceptable.

There are no hard and fast rules about this. Love is more important than keeping score. Healthy boundaries are vital—no one has the right to make you do anything in bed that you don't want to do, nor is anyone else responsible for your pleasure and satisfaction. We each need to speak up about what we want and what we don't want in bed.

In the case of sexual dysfunction—usually impotence in men and lack of orgasm in women—there are tried and true methods that can be employed to help individuals and couples, excellent manuals and books for information and, of course, trained professionals if consultation and therapy is required.

If a full sexual relationship is being prevented from prospering because one partner's inhibitions or insecurities are preventing it, the source of these it problems needs to be established. That individual or both partners can then seek appropriate help and treatment. There should be no blame or criticism, because sex is a very vulnerable area for most people and egos are fragile. Any kind of pressure will only exacerbate the problem. Sex should never be used for emotional blackmail, for example, using guilt to manipulate a desired result.

If there is addiction on the part of one or both partners in a relationship, it needs to be dealt with in the same way as any other problem. Understanding the addictive behaviour, tracing its source and owning the problem will keep the excesses under control and, with work, eliminate the exaggerated hunger altogether.

I can offer these guidelines, but we know that sex will still remain a major source of stress and fighting in marriage. Taken as a whole, this book can serve as a reference point to reduce these tensions. Relating is a skill like any other—it can be learnt, practised and, while never perfected, at least skilfully managed.

Sex is a life skill that should be taught in secondary schools, with lessons not only about condoms and AIDS, but also about all the things we're discussing in this chapter—intimacy, communication, true sexuality. Learning about sex is just as important as learning about history, maths or social studies. It's ignorance that results in unwanted pregnancy, premature sex, single mothers and sexually transmitted diseases, not information. Sex education needs to be addressed in the home as well.

As a society, we need to finally lay to rest our fears, taboos and prejudices in favour of freedom, enlightenment and knowledge. That doesn't mean we have no structure or values. Quite the contrary. I'm suggesting we put aside our meaningless, unnecessary hangups that were created by a generation which was hung up on guilt and Victorian ethics. Let us truly move into the twenty-first century by fostering true values based on joy and not punishment.

Casual sex is less lightly undertaken than it used to be in the 1960s and 1970s, which is ironic. Some people enjoy casual sex, claiming it's more exciting. It certainly is very different to marital sex. In what way?

Casual sex is freer, less complicated, both emotionally and practically. Marital sex is the type where, after you make love, you are just as likely to look up at the ceiling and say, 'Hey, that light globe needs changing.' You don't just go to bed as two individuals when you're in a committed relationship—you have money issues and possibly children and everyday problems and practical concerns. You're often tired, more often than not a cuddle is more attractive than intercourse and sex can start to feel like the last chore of the day.

That's why it's so important to have a whole range of ways to stay close in a marriage and not just rely on sex for closeness. Touching, massage, talking, walking together, holding hands, laughing—these are the threads that bind two hearts in a way that a quick fumble at the end of a long day can never do. Make time for sex less often but with more quality, when you can really enjoy each other's bodies and feel the love that brought you together in the first place. It's also important to have variety in your sexual activity as it's very easy for sex to become stale if you just do the same moves over and over. Use fantasy, sex aids, your imagination, explore, experiment, open your minds, discover your own bodies and share them with joy.

Emotional life

Emotional nourishment is as crucial as sexual satisfaction in a marriage. We tend to separate emotions into good and bad—love, kindness, joy, cheerfulness, peace are good, anger, fear, sadness, depression are bad. That's not true. Emotions are simply energy and as such, there is no judgement to be made of them. We feel them and, if allowed, they simply are released. If not, they stay in the body and cause stress, pain and even disease. Emotional nourishment is necessary on a daily basis. We each have an individual responsibility to seek balance, internal wellbeing, and relationship with self.

Once this is achieved, relationships of all kinds are easier, more comfortable and less likely to fail. If we allow ourselves solitude rather than isolation, moods rather than game-playing and manipulation, empowerment rather than codependence, if we look for the invisible signs of love everywhere and never give ourselves away to anyone, we begin to enjoy living in our own skins, walking our own paths. If you can just concentrate on walking your own journey, looking back a little but never with regret or anger, without looking too far forward, not looking to the left or the right, not getting distracted by what everyone else needs and wants, believing in your own dreams and never, never doubting yourself—that's immensely powerful.

❦

So many of us milk the past for comfort and the future for hope instead of living in the beautiful present where all is manageable and all is possible. When we look to the past, we often feel sad; when we look to the future, we often feel fear. But each moment of the present is perfect in its simplicity. I remind myself to live each day and each moment of my life fully and when I do, it works like a well-oiled machine. When I forget to trust, stay positive and stay in the present, I feel 'bad'. Love, joy, peace and infinite power resides within each of us, always available, if we only know it.

Accepting love from another, friendship, joy, life, ease, comfort, prosperity, health and all other good things requires self love and that's the stumbling block for most people. How can we allow ourselves the security and safety of being loved if we don't know deservability? It's much easier just to sabotage happiness, go from relationship to relationship, hang on to addictions, abandon friendship and hate ourselves. Happiness? Not likely.

6.
Before and After Relationships

WE CAN'T TALK ABOUT RELATIONSHIPS without mentioning the stress caused by the loss of love. This can happen in a number of ways: breakdown and breakup, death, geographical (physical) separation, family feuds and other conflicts. If a relationship such as a marriage or a long-term live-in arrangement becomes irretrievably damaged, counselling has been tried or rejected as a possibility, and the two parties decide to give up, there is a sense of loss, similar to a death, even for the one who may be keener to end things. Regardless of the issues and reasons, a process of grieving needs to take place. It's better if there can be a mutual decision to end the relationship, but if one person doesn't want to finish, there's tremendous strain and inbuilt resentment that permeates proceedings, especially if there was little or no warning.

As we know, an actual breakup can take months or even years, especially if there are things in common such as property or custody of children to settle. A relationship that ends in court or acrimoniously—or both—affects the parties for years to follow, which is why I always recommend that couples try to put aside their differences in order to part with love and dignity.

People often ask me how they can tell when there's no longer any hope in trying to patch up a relationship. The obvious signs—fighting and indifference, lack of caring, rudeness and so on—are not always immutable proof of the end. Even a dying marriage can be saved if both parties truly want it and are prepared to put the work in. I would love to see everyone make it, but when I recognise the danger symptoms, I accept that it's better for all concerned to call it a day. I advise people to ask themselves if the abuse being suffered is greater then the love being generated. That's a pretty good test. Don't let anyone tell you when to end a relationship or that you should do so. No outside person can judge what a relationship between two people is and often a third party has their own agenda. Timing is everything—you will know when the moment to go is right.

I am pro marriage. I certainly don't agree with giving up as soon as the going starts to get tough because you'll only bring the same problems up the road and marry someone else the same until you resolve the problems with yourself and your partner. A break-up may still be the result, despite your efforts, but at least you'll know you tried.

Staying together for the sake of the children can prove to be a false argument because if the children are being harmed by their parents' interaction then they too would be better off in a new environment. A trial separation can be a good idea as it allows time out and a defusing of tension, but it's important that certain ground rules are accepted and adhered to, for example, an approximate period agreed upon for the separation, rules on dating other people, seeing each other, continuing to have sexual relations or not, criteria for resuming the marriage. If these types of agreements are not put in place, what tends to happen is that one partner might simply wish to cancel the separation without any discussion or resolution and therefore, nothing is achieved. Alternately, both partners may want to resume the marriage, but if there's no understanding of the problems that caused them to break up, the same crisis point could be reached again.

Whether a relationship ends altogether or is suspended for a time, it's vital that the issues are aired and understood. Counselling can help because it offers an independent, impartial forum for discussion and improvement. If both parties are committed to positive change, there's no reason why the marriage can't survive and thrive.

Counselling can work well for other types of relationships, which, when they hit bad patches, can also be aided by judicious mediation. Family therapy, where whole families sit down together to honestly air their grievances and find better strategies for interaction, is now commonplace. Even if the problems don't disappear, everyone can feel empowered by the process and, as in the case of a married couple, if they decide to go their separate ways, they can at least resist the need for blame, anger and hatred.

Closure is crucial but often not possible until some time has elapsed and emotions have cooled. When two people can hug and wish each other well, letting go with love and warmth, then they can truly move forward into new lives and new relationships.

Of course, it isn't always desirable for one or both to do this. When this is the case, I suggest to the willing party to achieve closure on their own. This can be done by writing a letter of farewell in which you say goodbye to four separate things—the things you liked about the relationship, the things you didn't like, the dreams you had for the two of you and then, finally, the person him or herself. Then send the letter. A lot of pain can be released in this way but it's only effective when anger and bitterness has ended. Before that, you can write a venomous letter to your ex-partner, your parent, sibling or former friend, but I advise not sending this type, no matter how tempting it is. Burn it or tear it up as a symbolic gesture of release and forgiveness.

Forgiveness

This is a tricky area. So many people tell me they find it impossible to forgive the hurts they've suffered either at the hands of their parents or other family members, betraying friends or hurtful partners or lovers. I do understand, but the point is that forgiveness is more for you than the other person. Sure, forgiveness is a gift, but it benefits the giver far more because it is the beginning of healing. Until you have truly forgiven someone, you cannot completely heal. There's a good saying for this: 'Don't mark the place where the hatchet is buried.'

If you intend to keep remembering and bringing it up, you haven't really let it go, it is still a grudge in your heart and will affect your feelings about the person who hurt you. No matter how terrible the pain was or the let-down or the cruelty, try not to judge, as no one can ever really know another's heart.

If you decide to let someone out of your life because they have hurt you beyond acceptance, that's different. You can forgive someone and still not want to see them any more. Forgiveness does not mean self-abuse or being a martyr or taking whatever treatment is dished out. It's spirituality and self-loving that lifts you and blesses the other. It is so sad to hear of family members who haven't spoken to each other for years over some slight misunderstanding or a person holding a grudge that has festered and darkened over time—imagine the harm to your health when you hold on like that! Louise Hay goes so far as to suggest that cancers are caused by lack of forgiveness because we literally turn the hatred back onto ourselves.

Every night, I let go of all hurts, disappointments, grudges, disputes, arguments and anger of the day because I don't want to wake up the next day with all this negativity still in me. Think of the accumulation after a week, a month, a year, a lifetime. Without forgiveness, release and closure, we are guaranteed to bring this emotional baggage with us into the next relationship. Examining your part in a relationship with honesty and openness means you won't be doomed to repeat your mistakes and even if you do, you'll have a lot more awareness. Rushing out to find another partner simply to kill the pain of loneliness is the easy way out but less beneficial in the long term as you're quite likely to meet the wrong type of person in this way or, if it lasts, you'll probably find you've picked the same person again but with a different face. Falling in love on the rebound is never wise because it's caused by need and neediness rather than strength and self-love. Allow time to grieve and heal, a most necessary part of losing love and rebuilding your life. If a relationship ends chances are that your partner loved you too much or too little—either way, how does it matter if they don't want to be with you anymore? Once someone has left your bed and your life, what they do is largely irrelevant to you, isn't it, really? Be honest. The amount of energy we expend in torturing ourselves with regret, recrimination, replaying events, imagining scenarios, and so on is a complete waste. Most of us agree once the drama is over, so why not let yourself off that particular hook sooner rather than later?

Loneliness

Loneliness can be a time of great insight and growth: when the time is right, you'll emerge stronger and surer than ever.

Some pointers to help you deal with loneliness

- Loneliness is only a bad thing if you allow it to be. Being alone can be enjoyable.
- Don't rely on other people to keep you entertained. Develop your own interests.
- Keep in mind that everyone in the world is lonely at some time in their lives, even the most successful and famous person, even people in relationships.

- Keep busy, but don't just fill in time. Find activities that fulfil and satisfy you.
- Don't pretend to be busy when you're not, for example, by refusing invitations just to save your pride. You might miss out on really good opportunities.
- Reach out to other people. Make a phone call instead of complaining to yourself that you're alone and lonely.
- Don't waste energy and time envying others and feeling sorry for yourself. Enjoy being you.
- A bright, happy person is rarely lonely.
- It's possible to be lonely in a crowd. Inner strength prevents loneliness.
- Happiness is a condition, not a goal. Peace with oneself is lasting, not transitory.
- It is better to be lonely for a while than stay in a relationship that makes you unhappy.
- Discover all the wonderful things that life has to offer—nature, friends, art, music, your home, sports, games, etc.
- Allow yourself to be discouraged or depressed sometimes. It's all part of the human condition. Your true friends will accept you, moods and all.

Death and grieving

If your loss was through death, there may be other specific issues to work through. It will depend a lot on your religious views and whether you believe in life after death as to how you will deal with them. Let me share my views with you about this.

For me, death is 'going home', because I believe that we each have an eternal soul; therefore, dying is simply a step into another existence, not the end but a beginning, another adventure, a return to the completeness we all come from. That is, I believe, what the white light is that people who have experienced clinical death speak of. It is God, it is universal energy, heaven—I don't care what it's called. It is a place of total peace and the purest joy. I have experienced the white light in a meditation and it was like nothing I've felt elsewhere. It was unearthly, the white blinding in its intensity. I felt no fear whatsoever.

Death is only fearful because it is the great unknown, the final mystery of our time on earth but trust your own instincts instead of letting your imagination run wild with how horrible it's going to be or dreading the nothingness. It's much worse for the bereaved than the dead, so even in our pain, we need to recognise the selfishness of suffering. We mourn as much for ourselves as for the loved ones we've lost and that's okay as long as we don't martyr ourselves in the name of that pain and blame it on the deceased. I'm absolutely sure they don't want us to grieve and they pray only that we let them go to rest in peace.

The stages of grief after losing a partner are essentially the same, whether caused by physical death or death of a relationship.

> **The stages of grief**
>
> shock/numbness
> anger/bitterness
> denial
> release
> acceptance.

You will work through these in your own way and in your own time. No one can say how long that should take or how you should feel. Only you will know when it's over—and it could be years. You will still always remember and care about the person, but the memory will recede into the background of your life where it belongs. At first, it hurts too much to remember and at the same time, it hurts too much to forget, but gradually, with time, you make friends with the pain and memories will grow to comfort you instead of tearing you apart.

A well-known public figure who interviewed me tried to get me to say that love always turns to hate after a divorce or similar breakup. I couldn't agree as I have seen many cases where people break up because of incompatibility but they're still very much in love; even when warring couples say they hate each other, this is only the flip side of love. The apparent hatred is the face of love gone wrong. If love is ever present, it can never die, only transform. Even reconciliation is possible. I've seen all kinds of relationships transform miraculously when the people involved agree to honest self-appraisal and constructive change.

If each and every kind of relationship we have is viewed as gift that contributes to our healing and grow, as an important stepping stone, we would never say that a particular relationship was a waste of time or invest resentment where a person or situation failed to live up to expectations.

Some relationships are intrinsically stressful, such as those with, say, in-laws, step-parents and former partners. In the end, you'll basically like whoever you make up your mind to like. There's usually a power struggle between women and their mothers-in-law due to rivalry between them for the affections of the husband/son. To heal this, you just stop being rivals and work together as a team instead.

The same applies to ex-partners, particularly where there are children involved: you have to cooperate for their sake so you may just as well keep it pleasant as unpleasant. You always have a choice.

If the other person is 'impossible', you make it impossible for them not to get on with you. You like them till they like you back and if they still refuse, you accept them. You are never going to like everyone you're forced to deal with but you always have the choice of how your part of the interaction goes.

A sure way to prevent stress is to not compare yourself with anyone. If an ex-wife decides that a new wife is getting a better deal than she got, she'll resent it and look back on the relationship as being a failure instead of allowing that no two people interact the same—comparison is futile. Keep the good memories and discard the rest. It's not a matter of burying the truth, but the truth is relative—your perspective will not necessarily be the same as another's. Insisting that they agree with you is a waste of time.

Jealousy and envy also create a lot of bad feeling, particularly in the home and in the workplace. Just focus on what you're doing and leave others to worry about themselves. You'll find that your relationships will simplify that way and your life will be a lot less stressful.

The Single Life

Let's now turn our attention to those who have embraced the single lifestyle, regardless of reasons, whether it be short-term or long-term. It may seem out of place in a book about relationships to talk about the single lifestyle, but you may recall that I mentioned right at the beginning of this book that our discussion would not be confined to marital or love relationships, and that every person, no matter in what their circumstances, is dealing with relationships of several kinds every day. So, living-single people are still involved in the business of relationships.

One of the ways that men or women could find themselves living alone is by staying single, either by design or default.

If you are someone who lives this lifestyle, the only relevant question is—what attitude do you hold about it? Do you see being single as negative, an inferior lifestyle, something to be endured? If you do, your life will be an exercise in sheer frustration instead of the joyful experience it should be. Unfortunately, we live in a couple-oriented society and single people are frequently seen as unattractive people who no one wants anyway, overly fussy losers or sexually suspect weirdoes. Having taught a university course for eight years on the single life, I can truthfully say that there is no stereotypical single person. They come in all shapes, sizes, ages, personalities, looks and types, so if we look at what is supposed to be typical, we can see the unusual, the unorthodox, the beautiful.

Living as we do in a changeable, disposable society, many of us find ourselves single for some period in our lives, even if only for the time between relationships. Very few of us choose to be single for a whole lifetime, but those who do see it as a proud vocation and plan a life around pursuits other than marriage and children. The conventional route seems to just bypass some people and it's not difficult to wake up one morning and find yourself middle aged and alone.

This can happen even if you have married. That's why a lot of my work is centred around two main concepts—personal empowerment and having a relationship with oneself. The relevance of this theme is in always remembering that we have choices even when we appear not to and realising that you can never actually be alone because you always have you. In the light of the negative images society in general has and promotes about singles, it's vital to hold your own self-esteem firm, to know that you are valuable and, most important, complete—with or without a partner.

However long you are single and whether or not you like it, it's up to you to make it the most satisfying experience you can.

What do we even mean these days when we refer to someone as being 'single'? It used to be simple—a single person was an unmarried person, but these days there are several definitions. What about someone who's unmarried but dating steadily? What if you live with a partner without benefit of marriage vows? What if you have children and so don't live alone? It's a lot more complex an issue than it used to be.

For the purposes of this section, let's put aside all the possible reasons for the single state and focus on how it can be a positive experience.

> **So far, we've said**
>
> Don't buy into the stereotype.
> Be proud of being single.
> Don't ever see it as an inferior lifestyle.
> Let's move on from there.

What's good about being single? How can it be a positive rather than bitter experience?

What follows (page 128) are some of the pluses single people have pointed out to me over the years and that I've found to be so myself during the times in my life between relationships.

Of course we always have to be realistic about the not-so-good aspects, the obvious one being loneliness, although, as explained earlier in this chapter, there's no need for this to be a problem.

Okay, so nine out of ten people want to be in a permanent, loving relationship, but remember that a relationship is only preferable when it's positive and healthy. If it's not, it's far better to be alone. There is nowhere in existence more lonely than a marriage bed when two occupants no longer love each other; there's nothing more unromantic than divorce.

> ### Desirable aspects of being single
>
> - Autonomy over choices, activities, money, time, etc.
> - Freedom to do whatever is desired.
> - Time for personal growth, new hobbies, interests and friends.
> - More flexibility in schedules, comings and goings.
> - More scope—in a relationship, one's world can shrink and fall into a rut.
>
> ### Less desirable features of being single include
>
> - difficulties forming a social network
> - prejudices against single people, negative stereotypes
> - lack of intimacy and sharing with a special person
> - having to do everything yourself
> - not being able to take advantage of bulk discounts and special deals on travel and so on.

Never be desperate for love; needy vibes are a big turn-off. Love has a way of turning up when you least expect it. So, what do you do in the meantime to look after yourself?

Our needs

Mental

All human beings have certain needs that should be looked after on a daily basis, no less so by single people. These needs come under the following categories, though not necessarily in this order.

> **Our needs**
>
> Intellectual
> Emotional
> Physical
> Social
> Spiritual
> Material
> Sexual

In Western society, our intellectual needs are generally catered for by our professions. If you're in a job that is stimulating and creative, it's best to develop outside interests that balance this out, for example, light entertainment, popular novels, relaxing pursuits, sport, music and the like, while a job that is repetitive and dull needs to be combined with hobbies that stretch your mental abilities, such as using television, the internet and books for intellectual exercise, as well as conversation and discussions with others. The expression 'Use it or lose it' is particularly applicable to brain capacity. It's very easy for the mind to get lazy.

What constitutes emotional nourishment varies from person to person according to their temperament. People who feel deeply, have a lot of insight into their own psychological make-up and expend energy questioning behaviours and motives, is likely to look after themselves very well in this area. However, we should all be mindful of the importance of emotional wellbeing and the need for balance between this and other aspects of health.

Physical

Physical needs tend to demand the sort of attention that we already know about—from an early age we know that it's necessary to sleep, eat, use the toilet, rest, clean ourselves and so on—so these physical needs don't require a great deal of thought. In fact, we usually only think about the workings of our bodies when we're hungry, or need to go to the toilet, or when we feel ill or indisposed in some way.

Prevention is far better than cure and a life lived in moderation and balance will stop a lot of problems before they start, as dull as that might sound. My philosophy is that I'd rather look after myself in a general way than wait to get sick. If I'm well, I can do all the things I love in life, so moderation does not have to mean a dull existence. Quality and quantity are what I'm after, not just a quick patch of overindulgence followed by years of regret.

It's possible to be overly concerned about your health, which is actually unhealthy. Some people put a tremendous effort into caring for their physical fitness, which is fine, as long as not overdone.

Material

Material needs are a roof over our heads, sufficient clothing for our purposes and an even flow of financial incomings and outgoings. A simple rule of thumb is to keep a balance between what you spend, what you save, the number of financial commitments you have and your security concerns. Spending everything you earn is not good, but nor is putting away too much for the future.

Money is a currency and the name tells you it should move. Holding on too tightly can create a poverty consciousness, in other words, fears about lack and insecurity. Money is just a commodity and should never be endowed with emotional qualities. It can never make you happy but having enough of it certainly makes life easier so aim for maximum income, more income than outgoings, and learn to enjoy money in the process.

Spiritual

Spiritual needs are largely neglected in our society, mainly because of a lack of understanding about what it means to be spiritual and also because most people equate spiritual with religious. Organised religion will always have its role to play, but in recent years many have turned to alternative practices, for example, the New Age movement and Eastern religions such as Buddhism which are less orthodox and rigid in their practice.

Does not wanting to be religious at all preclude you from being spiritual? Not in my view. As far as I'm concerned, each one of us has an immortal soul, which is our essence, our perfect centre, and which does not have to be expressed in order to be present. To access this spirit, it is not necessary to do anything other than be, be open and allow it to flow through us, empowering us in many ways and enriching our lives. This can be aided by music, poetry, nature, and a love of people, animals and places. It is really just about having a relationship with self—unfortunately, something most people aren't very good at. Yet to feel one's own inner power is the beginning of all true self-esteem and the foundation for peace and joy in life.

Singles need to develop a healthy attitude to sexual needs and self-pleasuring, to take responsibility for personal sexual needs and to broaden their concepts of sexuality beyond genitals, intercourse and orgasm (see, especially, chapter 7). Sexuality is far more than that and can be expressed through creative pursuits, many different forms of love, a wider notion of intimacy, friendship and connection with nature. Sexuality is linked to the lifeforce energy along with creativity, spirituality, love and joy—all of these are present within us always so there is never any need to feel a lack of one or more of these components in our lives.

You can never be without love because you are love; you carry it always with you. You can never be alone because you always have yourself and you need never fear sexual frustration because there are many ways for this to be expressed, not just one.

Social networks

Now, the big one for singles—building a social network. Why is it so difficult? Many divorced singles complain about losing friends in the separation process, some say they no longer get invited to the same parties as before, and the most common cry—where does one go to meet nice members of the opposite sex?—is heard time and time again The first two relate to the prejudices we spoke of before but you can certainly do something about the last point.

Building a social network is no different to building a business network. It's a slow and instinctual process that requires confidence and patience. Just like a bricklayer building a house, brick by brick the structure grows until it's strong enough to stand.

If this all sounds a bit too much like hard work, here's my best and simplest advice—go out! Just once. It doesn't matter where or what to—just accept one invitation, join one group, turn up at one party. From the tiny acorn the mighty oak grows. You'll meet someone who'll have a network of their own and more ideas will generate, more friends will be met, more places will turn up to try and so forth.

Is it easy? No, mainly because of the fear of failure, fear of looking foolish. If you go out specially to meet a lover, you will be disappointed as this will rarely happen, if ever. But go out to meet new friends—of both sexes—and you can only win. Your attitude to the whole experience will be different and you'll be more likely to find success. Someone special might tap you on the shoulder at one of these occasions, but it's best if you're not looking out for that special one too much as you might miss all the fun in the process.

My best recommendation is interest groups where you will at least be sure of meeting like-minded people. Whatever you're into, there's a group for you—Scrabble, bushwalking, bootscooting, films, travel, wine. You can also enrol in classes that teach subjects you're interested in or take personal development courses that will enrich your self-knowledge and life skills. Dinner clubs are a very civilised way for you to try out a variety of restaurants and meet a small group of mixed singles who will hopefully provide interesting dinner conversation if nothing else. Social groups of all kinds abound in our cities: ask around before you join or go along to one of the trial evenings.

Finding the mate

If you're really serious about finding a mate and you want to formalise the procedure, you can join an introduction agency. Here are some tips from a very experienced matchmaker.

A matchmaker's tips

- You pay for what you get so it's best to join one of the pricier agencies where you'll get better service.
- The person who interviews you is unlikely to be the one who matches you so be very clear upfront on what your requirements are.

> - Ask exactly what you can expect from the company—weekly updates, two dates a month, etc.
> - Don't fall for the $1 deposit and sign up ploy—you might find that even that tiny deposit constitutes a binding agreement.
> - Shop around—don't be shy about it. Do not sign on the dotted line until you've compared agencies and decided on the agency that best suits your needs.

Obviously, there is no shortage of ideas on how to get out and have a good time but it's up to you to decide to take a chance and keep an open mind. If you decide it's hopeless, it will be; if you wait for others to make overtures, you could be old and grey before you ever go out again. The best story I have about this point comes from an older chap in one of my classes.

He took himself off to a well-known stamping ground for singles, sat at a small table, ordered a drink and then sat and sat, feeling isolated and out of his depth. He was just about to give up and leave when a woman called out his name. When he looked around, he saw a woman he knew slightly who had arrived with a female friend. They joined him and others came along who also sat down. The second woman moved over next to him and, after they talked for a while, they found that they had a lot in common, including golf. The next thing—they had made several arrangements to do things together. When my student recounted the story, he emphasised that he was not interested in the woman romantically, but by taking himself out, he had widened his circle and met a nice new companion.

It's a good lesson for us all.

Internet dating

One of the ways that people are reaching out to each other in the twenty-first century is through internet dating. The anonymity of these contacts lends them a certain air of mystique, but this process has some inherent dangers that are uniquely related to the internet.

We all want everything so fast today, and the world is getting smaller due to the swiftness of communications. Those of us who use computers can reach out to anyone, anywhere in the world. Out in cyberspace, we can be anything we want, and there's a temptation to gild the lily. A nerdy young man can say he's Tom Cruise, Superman and Sylvester Stallone all rolled in one; a shy plain woman can be Marilyn Monroe or Madonna in looks and sex appeal. Why not?—no one can see you. You're just lines on a screen and even if photos are exchanged, they don't have to be genuine.

So, does that mean that we shouldn't write to strangers on the net or participate in chatroom discussions? Not at all. In safer times, people had pen friends for years with whom they exchanged addresses and other personal details. These days it is not wise to give out that sort of information on the net because it's too easy for it to be leaked. Besides, even the person you're writing to may be a risk. It's sad, but true.

The answer is not to be paranoid or overly suspicious but to simply exercise commonsense and be reasonably cautious.

The benefits of meeting others on the net are accessibility, convenience, freedom, choice, communication and dispelling loneliness. It's the singles' venue of the twenty-first century, and the place for bored marrieds, especially sex chatrooms.

There's no need for anyone to be lonely at any time of the day or night, 365 days of the year. But there's also more potential for romantic illusion on the internet. It's easy to talk yourself into believing that the person you're writing to is everything you've ever dreamed of, the perfect Mr or Ms Right. It's the same danger in all new relationships—that the initial attraction is mistaken for true love. How much easier this is in electronic romance where everything is removed from the senses except the imagination—which can create anything it wishes. There are none of the usual safety checks, no intuitive guide, no touching or looking into eye, no body language to watch or tone of voice to hear—just the mind and an image of and yearning for the desired lover. The very style of internet communication makes it feel warm and intimate, being undertaken as it is in your own home, so it's easy to get sucked into that cosy world and ignore the warning signals.

A less positive interpretation of internet dating is that it caters for those unable to commit to a normal, everyday relationship—romance addicts, for instance, who only want magic, newness and excitement, fantasy addicts who can't cope with real life, the commitment phobics who are terrified of true intimacy and emotional responsibility. If you are indulging in internet relationships because real, flesh-and-blood ones frighten you, then you need to reexamine your motives and find the courage to face the challenge of personal interaction. If you are afraid of committing to a relationship fully, you might keep falling for unavailable people such as those who are already married, those who live at a considerable distance from you, those who travel for a living or those with whom you have only internet communication. Think about it.

My advice regarding internet dating would be this—have fun, meet lots of people, share knowledge and information, use all the facilities this wonderful medium has to offer, but do not let your guard down. Don't give up your job, home and friends to fly half way around the world to meet someone you've met on the net. If they are in the same city as you, arrange a personal meeting in a public place, the same as you would any other blind date. Writing to someone for months or even years gives you a false sense of intimacy but the cases where two people can meet under these circumstances and find lasting and true love would be very rare.

So, keep those rose-coloured glasses snapped firmly away in the spectacles case but your heart always open to life's possibilities.

7. Relationship With Self

IN THIS LAST CHAPTER, I am offering you a range of tools and skills to use to make practical improvements to your life situations, and to your relationships in every area of life—your closest relationships as well as your dealings with acquaintances, enemies and strangers.

I'm going to begin with a subject that most people think of as abstract and unattainable and yet it's probably the one thing we all say we want—happiness. It is not impossible or unrealistic to want to be happy, in fact, it is with you in every moment of your existence: you only have to reach for it to find it within yourself. The problem with happiness is that it is surrounded by myths that we've accepted to be the reality, thus limiting our real experiences of joy, peace, love, laughter—all the feelings we associate with happiness.

Without personal joy, your relationships will remain co-dependent or be continually in conflict, perhaps both. So let's look at the myths surrounding happiness and see about dispelling them.

Myths about happiness

> **Most people believe that happiness:**
> - comes from outside themselves
> - is associated with a person, thing, event or circumstance
> - is not possible for human beings to hold on to
> - is in the future, a goal we have to work towards
> - has to be given to us by someone
> - has to be earned
> - is always followed by unhappiness.

Let's take a look at these myths one by one.

Myth #1—Happiness comes from outside ourselves

I believe that happiness is a state of being and is, therefore, part of our essence in the same way as our lifeforce, creativity and sexuality are. Happiness, like our internal power can be accessed at any time; they are limitless, like an eternal spring within us. If you're not feeling happy at this moment while reading this book and you're inclined to dismiss what I'm saying, just think for a minute how liberating it would be if you didn't ever have to do another thing in order to be happy. You just are and you will be for ever in a continuous stream.

The reason people resist this idea is because they misunderstand the nature of happiness. It isn't about laughing and cheering and partying all day; although these activities are manifestations of happiness, they're not happiness itself. It sometimes seems clearer to speak of joy, as the word 'happiness' evokes so many different images for different people. Feel the peace and harmony deep inside you—that's the place where your joy resides. Please don't ever say you don't have it as that would be denying your very centre.

I met the concept of continuous happiness with as much scepticism as most people would because I too always believed that happiness is supposed to be fleeting and life full of ups and downs. Once I had been introduced to these new ways of looking at life a few years ago, it took a lot of unlearning and patience and releasing of old patterns but now I can honestly say that whether I have a partner or not, money or not, whether it's sunny or rainy, whether I am working or playing, I am happy—not ecstatic or high, but happy in my own skin, at peace with myself and my world, glad to be alive and appreciating each day's adventure. Although I am a cheerful person by nature, I used to be a control freak, a stressaholic and workaholic; I was fearful and felt unlovable underneath a confident and strong exterior. All that has changed because I do love myself now, so I'm not as concerned with others' opinions. I have many bright reflections all around me which mirror my own state of being.

How do you do it? As with everything else, you must first have the desire. After that there's the know-how; that's where I come in. We'll continue to look at the myths about happiness and that is a beginning because when you let go of outdated ideas and attitudes, you have a fresh palette on which to paint a new picture, your own picture, choosing the colours you want and the scenery, and whether it's bright or dull. In this way, you do create your existence moment to moment and are no longer a victim of life.

By either trying to control everything or feeling powerless, you can never find that centre of joy because it becomes blocked; you could easily live an entire lifetime not even realising it's there.

Okay, so that takes care of myth number 1—happiness is not outside you, it can never be given by another person and you don't have to get it.

Myth #2—happiness comes from acquiring objects

If you attach the idea of happiness to a particular object and make the two things synonymous, then, logically, you cannot have one without the other. Thinking that happiness is a car, a trip, a lover, a job, money in the bank, a house or whatever means that if you haven't got this item, you feel you're not happy. There's nothing wrong with wanting these things, but just don't attach your happiness factor to them. You are happy just because you are and for no other reason.

Myth #3—happiness is elusive

Happiness is something we have to work towards, an elusive goal and it's nature is mercurial; no sooner do we feel happy than it's taken away.

Happiness is actually sustainable at an even level all the time. You might miss the exciting highs and the debilitating lows but in the long term, you will be grateful for the daily gift of inner peace, instead of being buffeted by the winds of change and feeling at the mercy of life's vagaries.

Remember, everything around you reflects your state of mind and emotional health in the moment. So, if you don't like your reflections, you can set about changing them instantly. If you're fully attuned to your happiness, your reflections will be bright—car, house, money, health, job, relationships. The point is to have it the right way around—when you're happy, you will have the things you want in life, not when you have the things you want, you'll be happy. That's the fundamental mistake our society makes—we look for reasons to support our feeling good as if we need an excuse, a rationalisation to cover up our guilt over being happy. We are not generally good at being happy yet it's hardly a skill to be mastered. It is our birthright; as we've seen before, every baby is born into this world naturally happy until the joy in it is killed by adults who don't understand this.

If you see happiness as a goal to be reached in the distant future then it will always be out of your reach. Just remember, though, that you carry it around with you all the time and it's yours without having to be earned or paid for.

Myth #4—happiness has to come to us from someone else

No one else can ever make you happy or give you happiness. Expecting that they can is of course one of the main causes of relationship struggle and breakdown. If you enter a relationship believing that your happiness is someone else's responsibility then you will either be inviting disappointment or you will choose someone who wants to be codependent. When you are a complete, happy person, you can only share happiness, never give it. For years, I thought it was my fault if people around me weren't happy. I could never understand why. It took me a lot of years and heartache until I understood that each of us must find happiness in their own heart.

Myth #5—happiness has to be earned
When things are going well in our lives, we wait for the axe to fall, for punishment to follow. This is based on childhood conditioning caused by the retreat of natural joy. I say 'retreat' because our natural joy is not actually lost; it just gets locked away, sometimes—if we don't take steps as adults to rediscover it—forever. If and when you do recover your natural joy, you will feel the undiluted, pure joy of a child, no matter what your age. It is liberating and exhilarating, the start of a new life.

Myth #6—happiness can't last
When you make the commitment to live your life with joy, you have to let go of all your old belief systems surrounding happiness. Being happy all the time sounds so good, so why wouldn't we all volunteer to try it? Because the unknown is always scary. Unhappiness we know, it's familiar, but to accept continuous happiness as a daily reality is too good to be true.

Our society is riddled with these limiting ideas and concepts and we swallow them without question—but you don't have to!

Living with joy and in joy means a life without barriers, judgement, limitations or fear. Everything becomes joyful, even the most mundane tasks because your focus changes.

You will experience life intensely, the way a child does, see the beauty in small things, express your feelings openly without fear, love everything and everyone, most importantly, yourself. Too good to be true? How do you know until you try it? I can only tell you it's possible, even easy, once you decide to do it.

Bliss

This way of living is what I understand Joseph Campbell to mean when he suggest you 'follow your bliss'. It is a philosophical construct that I translate very simply to mean living in childlike joy. For example, if you feel the urge to take a half day off to go to the beach or the cinema, you follow it; if you feel the urge to hug someone, you do it; if you are reading a book or working or gardening, you totally absorb yourself in that activity and enjoy it to the hilt. In this way, your whole life becomes blissful and no longer divided into compartments of unpleasant, necessary jobs and pleasurable, desirable activities. It's all just life and it's all good.

You might think this is all airy-fairy nonsense but please recall my background—academic, achievement-oriented, left-brain, rational, workaholic, stressaholic, chronically ill, a control freak and disillusioned because I couldn't understand why, even though I was trying so hard, life felt so difficult.

That was precisely the problem—I was trying too hard. I could no more take time off during the week than fly to the moon. I only felt safe when I was working and even though that gave me a lot of satisfaction, I depleted myself working and giving and trying. There was no room for joy. Now, I have no room in my life for anything but joy. Everything I do is joy. It is just a shift of attitude and a self-loving decision to change.

Bliss is a state of being and it's a lot easier than being miserable but it's your choice and this choice is made from where you are in your life right now—are you self-loving or self-defeating? Make that choice first and the rest will follow.

Bliss is where you are; you don't have to go anywhere to find it but you can follow where it leads and live your life by trust and joy instead of suspicion and fear. Living in bliss involves what I call the 'wow factor', an attitude of excitement that means saying Wow! to life, even when it throws you an unexpected challenge. Imagine yourself to be a small child let loose in a sweet shop—that's what a blissful life is like, full of discovery, nice surprises, spontaneity, enthusiasm and interest. It may not all be equally desirable—even in a sweet shop you have your preferences—but you can sample and choose, taste and savour. Life's just an adventure anyway so why take it all so seriously?

My favourite saying, which sums everything I understand about happiness, goes like this:

There is no way to happiness; happiness is the way.

Prosperity

The first time I heard someone lecture about prosperity I was astounded because the philosophy being expounded was one I had always tried to live by, which caused me to be accused of being a Pollyanna, seeing life through rose-coloured glasses, being too emotional.

Here was a woman talking about prosperity as the most natural thing in the world and listing books written about the subject! It took me many years past that starting point to fully read, research and digest this way of living and thinking and even longer to actually begin living it fully. Even though I was, like everyone else at the lecture, by nature very receptive to the ideas I had a lot of unravelling and unlearning to do. I will try to share with you now some of the ideas of this philosophy as I understand it and I hope that I can encourage you to try them out for yourself.

Like me, you may feel as if this is a homecoming for you, or you may be initially resistant. If you feel the latter, it's probably because it sounds too easy and wonderful. As I've said repeatedly in this book, we humans are very wary of any idea that doesn't sound difficult or painful.

First of all, prosperity is not just about financial abundance, although that can be part of it. It is an overall attitude that life is good, a gift, and that it should be easy and fun.

Sounds foreign, doesn't it? When you laughed and played up as a child, did your parents say it's great that you're happy? They were probably more likely to say something like, 'What have you got to be happy about?' That's where we first absorb the idea that we need a reason to be happy. But then we're told that life is hard, so it follows that a reason is unlikely to be found. If you turn that around and work from the premise that life is easy and you're already happy, things start to change. Remember, life always supports your belief system so whatever you believe, you will basically experience.

Prosperity becomes evident in those reflections I've spoken

about—they are your living proof of the prosperity in your mind and heart. It has to start with you, and once it does, it will translate into material form. So, when you are ready to embrace a life of prosperity, you will see it in your body, work, money, relationships, home life, family and day-to-existence.

Obviously, none of this is possible without belief and desire which stem from self-love and trust. Say Yes, I am ready, then watch it start to happen. Of course, there is work to be done, but mainly on yourself. The key area is releasing fear and negative thinking because these two things alone will directly work against prosperity thinking, which is the exact opposite of limitation thinking, what we call poverty consciousness, a belief in lack and struggle.

Positive thinking is a choice and way of life which holds that there is a bright side to every situation and that it's only your perspective you have any power over so you can just as easily see the glass as half-full as half-empty. Even in the most tragic circumstance there can be a plus, a gain, a gift. Prosperity thinking goes even further; it is proactive rather than reactionary. It is based on self-loving behaviour that creates (key word!) a prosperous life. There's only acceptance of it; there's no need to work hard obtain it. In fact, once you open your mind, your heart and your arms to this new life, you can relax, let go and begin to really enjoy life without all the old fears, limitations and problems.

Tools to work with

There are specific tools to aid you along this path when you take your first ginger steps, still locked in the old ways, expecting failure, rejection, even humiliation. Affirmations are a very powerful tool that can literally brainwash you by cleansing your mind of its outdated, crippling thoughts, ideas and beliefs. They take time but most definitely work.

Affirmations

In order to make statements about yourself and your life and where you want to be in the future, you have to affirm them in the present. There are guidelines for using affirmations to maximise their effectiveness and minimise the time you have to wait for results.

For maximum effectiveness

- Use 'I'; you cannot affirm for another person.
- Affirm in the present tense.
- Keep the statements very specific.
- Write your own affirmations if you can.
- Keep your affirmations simple.
- Say or write your affirmations frequently.
- Work with a particular issue as needed, such as money, health, spiritual life.
- Allow time for these beliefs to take hold.

On the subject of results, you need a lot of patience because after all, you might be undoing a whole lifetime's conditioning. It's not going to happen overnight. Also, I find that as with the proverbial kettle that won't boil is you wait for it, results don't tend to come when you're waiting either, or they seem to take longer. If you wait to see brighter reflections in your life, you will usually be disappointed. That's the letting go and trusting bit again. It takes as long as it takes.

Control is such a difficult personal issue and it strongly affects relationships, particularly partner to partner and parent to child. When and how are particularly elusive in our daily quests so the best thing you can do when you want something is to put out for it in the form of a wish, affirmation or 'prayer', then just forget it and get on with life. I write 'prayer' here in inverted commas because there's traditional prayer but there's also communicating with the universe which is a little more general and less tied to religious belief; there's also sending blessings which is like praying for others, particularly effective for those who are unwell or in distress.

Always examine your true motives for what you want, too, as if your heart is not pure, for example, if you wish a person harm or send hatred to a person who has harmed you, you will not get what you want or, if you do, it will bring you no joy.

Prosperity, then, is essentially about living with love, not romance or marriage or even family; it's a wider emotion, encompassing everything and everyone we share the earth with. When you love yourself, you will love others, when you love, you'll automatically be happy and when you're happy, you'll be prosperous.

Sometimes when I say this, people argue that lots of good, loving people lead terribly tragic and sad lives. The answer to this is that they're not loving themselves. They may have genuine motives but perhaps they're prey to victim thinking or poverty consciousness or martyr behaviour, or they simply give too much in a misguided fervour of self-sacrifice. That's why I say be totally honest with yourself every day in what you do, feel, say and think—be your own truth monitor and you won't go wrong. Use your intuitive powers as suggested earlier in the book and let them guide you.

Creative visualisation
If you are more of a visual person than a words person, you might prefer to work with creative visualisation, which is a method of creating in your mind's eye the pictures or images of your desires and the life or specific things you want. Let's say you have a lifelong dream to own a red Mercedes. You could meditate on a vision of this object each day until you get it. Your visualisation needs to be very specific—a wishy-washy wish has no chance. Imagine yourself sitting inside the car: smell the upholstery, feel the steering wheel, see the car in your driveway with you sitting inside it. Engage all your senses to make the experience real.

In addition, surround yourself with pictures of this car, cut from magazines or sales brochures—stick them everywhere in your house so that you are literally absorbing the symbolism of this desired object as you move around and do your normal things. In one case I heard of, a man painted the rear of a car he wanted onto the surface of his rolladoor so that each time he pulled into his drive, he saw the back of the car in front of him as if it were already his and present. This may be a bit extreme but this type of blueprinting works. You can do the same for a dream home, lover, job, anything at all.

The only essential ingredient is belief. You have to affirm, visualise and 'pray' as if what you want is already yours. It's good to start each day with a prayer and/or blessing of thanks, joy and love. At the other end, it's good to let the day go and to once again give thanks for all that you have experienced, even the 'bad' stuff. Thankfulness is another tool of prosperity because you are acknowledging what you already have, focusing on your blessings rather than your lacks or wants. This in turn creates more abundance for you.

Expectation without demand also helps. Once you've asked, you rest in your total faith and stop stressing out about it—if you want more money, you ask for what you need, do what you can to improve your earnings or stretch your budget, then let it go. Worrying about money or anything else only makes it worse. In a relationship situation, you do your share then ask your own inner guidance to do the rest. I don't want you to get the impression that I'm saying you don't have to lift a finger in life and riches will come pouring in your front door. You still hold all the power of choice but you also allow that events have their own energy and rhythm; when you try to fix everything, you interrupt the natural flow and often push away the very things you want.

Wishing

Making wishes and expecting magic is difficult for people in Western societies. We despise people who appear to have it made, who appear to have it easy, who work in jobs they love, live off pensions and allowances, become hugely successful and wealthy. In Australia, for example, we admire the battler, a man or woman who worked hard all their life and has nothing or little to show for their efforts.

Why? Why shouldn't we work easy and have everything? Only because we don't ask for it and we don't ask for it because we don't think we deserve it. Without deservability, we are doomed to a life of struggle and unhappiness. If your core belief is that you have to work hard because that's noble and you're a better person if you're poor because that's noble too, then these will continue to be your realities. To change them is as easy as changing your mind and you need to do this literally. Free your mind and you'll free your life. I'm speaking very generally in this chapter, but everything I'm saying is directly applicable to relationships.

Wishing is positive thinking and affirmation of prosperity. When you buy your next lottery ticket, say to yourself as you pay for it, 'Thank you that I've won.' Expect to win. If you don't, why buy a ticket?

Another common saying is, 'God helps those who help themselves', so even if you are a traditional Christian or belong to another religion, you can still practise this philosophy I'm describing. I believe that God is inside me, part of me in energy and spirit; therefore, he's in everything else, not just in a church or in 'heaven'. I prefer to make my heaven here on earth because I believe that 'god' wants us all to be happy, not miserable, and that if we're miserable, it's our own fault. We have to have the courage to ask for what we want and expect to get it without whimpering and whining about our problems and hoping for anything, including God, to fix them for us.

This idea is likely to be controversial but I do not say it to be controversial. I sincerely believe that many people now are turning to alternative religion or belief systems because they no longer want to be told what to do, how to think and how to live their lives. Each one of us is a perfect soul and perfectly capable of living on this planet in whatever capacity we choose, which may include being an alcoholic homeless person. That is an individual's right and not one of us is allowed to say that our way is better.

I abhor self-righteousness above all else, probably because I used to practise it. Answer only to yourself and be true to yourself at all times. Do not justify your behaviour or explain yourself because that never works anyway. If you try, you will only be attempting to ingratiate yourself with those whose opinions you don't value and devaluing yourself in the eyes of those who do matter, most particularly yourself.

Dreams

You can have waking dreams or dreams that are messages from your subconscious, that come to you during sleep. The latter help us to release fears, anxieties, anger, longings, all sorts of emotions, thus refreshing us for life when we're awake.

Who's to say which is real? If you tend to avoid thinking about harsh realities during the normal course of your existence, it's possible that you will not remember your night-time dreams. You can choose, for instance, whether or not to experience nightmares. Dreamers who frequently have nightmares tend to be experiential people who enjoy loving life on the edge and embrace it all. At the extreme other end of the spectrum are those who will tell you they don't dream at all because, in fact, they are cut off from their own interior life. Everyone dreams, several times every night, the only difference being in the level of recall. Current dream research serves to illustrate more and more how thin the veneer is between subconscious and conscious mind.

Spirituality

We need to recognise our divinity if we are to be truly prosperous, so let's be clear as to what spirituality is and how it links to prosperity.

I believe that we are eternal souls encased in physical bodies so that we could come to earth to fulfil our destinies. Death is a homecoming rather the end of all existence (see chapter 5). I do not believe in the traditional concepts of heaven and hell, reward and punishment, but rather in the soul's immortality and autonomy. We are each a perfect being, even if we do many imperfect things which, of course, we do.

If you can accept the continuity of existence then you will understand that you can never be unspiritual any more than you can be unsexual or unhuman. Spirituality, sexuality, humanity just are; our own choice is whether to open ourselves up to them or not. When we do, we begin to experience our own divinity and our connection to everything and everyone else.

Spiritual love is not the same as personal love, which is selective and conditional. Universal love is all-encompassing and freely given to all without seeking reciprocation. If you practise this type of communion with others, it will benefit all your relationships, not just the closest ones. But most of all, it will benefit you because if you feel spiritually beautiful, you will see how illogical it is to hurt yourself—you will finally become your own best friend and protector. And this in turn will create prosperity in your life.

Creating prosperity is one thing; allowing it and living it is something else. I have created an 'ideal world' for myself several times, notably in 1981 and again in 1993. The first time I felt my own power, I went out and got all the magical things I'd ever wanted—bought a beautiful house near the river on a prayer and a promise, met a sexy new lover, had creative work and a high income. One by one, I lost each of them and a lot more throughout that year. I learnt my lessons, regrouped, moved forward until, in 1994, I stood much in the same position. An analogy I might use is feeling as if you're in an oasis, suspended from cares, obstacles, struggle; everything's in place and you feel that life is rewarding you for all your efforts and hard work. Between January and April of 1995, I systematically dismantled all that I had established in my life that was so perfect.

With the wisdom of hindsight, I now realise why that was necessary, but at the time, I felt that I had been self-defeating and self-sabotaging. I simply did not have deservability. What right had I to such happiness? Keep in mind that these are not rational thoughts but irrational, subconscious feelings. To be happy, you need to know you are and to accept your right to be.

Now, I am once again in a similar situation and I feel very comfortable with my success and prosperity, but I still affirm each day to keep my thoughts and my life positive.

When your life takes a prosperous turn, start looking out for two things: signposts and manifestation.

Signposts

Signposts are intuitive and practical messages all around you that present themselves in order to lead you along the life path that is right for you. If you are still into control and denial, you will miss them and continually create limitation, struggle and difficulties for yourself.

Signposts come in many forms—things people say to you, ideas, insights, something you read, lyrics of songs, your own writings, dream messages and so on. I'm not suggesting you read deep meaning into every stimulus or every bit of input into your life each day, but just don't dismiss them, especially if you start to notice a recurring pattern, for example, if you're going through a relationship crisis and everywhere, you seem to be surrounded by messages about your situation. Listen, tune in, as there might be an insight or even breakthrough to be gained. That's why you need a lot of time to heal after difficult patches in your life. Insights are hard-won and often come when you have laid down your weapons and given up the fight. You are not defeated as you are still open to the learning experience.

Manifestation

Manifestation is the physical, tangible evidence of your new thinking, attitudes, ideas and beliefs. As you change, your life will change and you should be able to see the living proof, the reflections showing you this. Don't watch and wait for them impatiently; keep your eyes open.

Manifestations may come in very slow, subtle forms or, in some cases, show up in dramatic, radical ways, such as a 'hopeless' situation turning around 'miraculously' or a person you'd given up on behaving positively towards you. Be thankful, revel in these successes without smugness or complacency, and prosperity will multiply. Again, I'm not saying these things idly. I have lived every stage of these experiences that I write about. You can consciously manifest too. It definitely works but only if you are not coming from control. Even an idle thought, such as 'I wish Mary would phone me', becomes reality after a bit of practice of allowing this power you possess. If you put all your positive energy into it, you can meet the perfect partner, get that dream job, heal rifts, win the lottery—whatever you want.

Just remember, don't try to control the how and the when. Don't let negative thinking and a lack of self-belief hold you back. If you feel you're banging and banging on a door that refuses to open, it could be that you're trying at the wrong door, that the timing is out or, somehow, you're doing it the wrong way. The best strategy is to walk away and either try later, in a different way or, better still, let the door spring open by itself. It will if you believe it will. Florence Scovel-Shinn says you must have 100 per cent faith in yourself and in life. That sounds like an impossible feat for humans but like everything else, it can be attained with patience and practice.

Mind power

Your mind is infinitely powerful, that is, without limit, immeasurable. How can anything stop you if you even harness a small percentage of that power. Don't wait till life forces you to reach for inner strength; use it every day to improve your experience of living and create more joyful circumstances for yourself. People often say to me that getting a major disease or having a near-fatal car accident woke them up to the precious gift of life, made them change from negative to positive. Don't wait and don't hand over your power to anyone, whether they be partners, parents, priests, doctors, politicians or advisors like me! Adapt everything you are told to your own personal situation because you are perfectly capable of running your own life and making your own decisions.

Whenever I feel bad, I know I've forgotten to do one or all of the following:

---

trust

stay positive

live in the present.

Armed with these three tools, life is always manageable, but I want a lot more than manageable for you and myself—I want it all! Let your life be filled with the wow factor.

Expect to be pleasantly surprised. Laugh a lot and sing and

dance. Allow room in your life every day for play, not just on weekends and holidays. Develop a mindset of play and let it permeate your thinking and your daily life.

I used to say that the most important thing to leave behind when you die is a legacy, be it good works, children, community service, creative works or whatever. I have now revised this opinion. The most important question I want to be able to answer in the affirmative when I'm on my deathbed is—Did I have fun? Did I enjoy the journey?

A woman, older than me, who was my second mother, died last year. She didn't die with her music 'still inside her'. Throughout her life she sang, played the piano, loved to cook for casts of thousands and did, married three times, bossed everyone around, laughed a lot, lived life to the full. As I watched her in bed, close to death, I thought to myself—I bet she'd say she had a great time.

Never say 'I can't', though you're entitled to say 'I don't want to' or 'I don't know how—yet'. Give yourself permission to grow or you never will. No one can do it for you. Besides, whether you permit yourself or not, life will force growth upon you and you probably then won't like it.

Here are some positive affirmations you might like to work with to get you started on a more prosperous life. Start the day by affirming that it's a perfect day before you've experienced any of it. Remember, your thoughts create your reality.

The affirmations that follow are very general; the most effective affirmations are the ones you write yourself on specific matters.

> **Try these affirmations**
>
> - All things are possible for me now.
> - I prosper in all things.
> - All is well in my world always.
> - I experience magic in my life every day.
> - I enjoy perfect health.
> - All my relationships are joyful and positive.
> - I look forward to a future that is bright, joyful and secure.

In regard to relationships, they can be either a source of great joy for you or great frustration and unhappiness. You may not believe it when I say that it's in your hands, but experiment with some of the ideas in this book and see the difference.

Above all, don't let negative thinking, self-doubt, past hurts, defensiveness or fear keep you from experiencing the joy that healthy relationships can add to your life and note that I say 'add', not 'give'.

I read recently that animals don't have a reality beyond the next moment, for example, a cat doesn't sit in its yard worrying about the dog two houses down breaking down the gate and attacking it. Think about it—isn't that exactly what we do? We worry and make real all the things that can and might go wrong for us down the track, thereby diluting the pleasure of the moment in the present.

Also, be watchful that your relationships do not die from neglect. Never be too busy to stop for a kiss and a hug from your partner or to play with your child or be there for a friend. You only get back what you put into life and nowhere is that truism more evident than in your relationships. If you do not like the look of the relationships you're currently experiencing, turn your gaze within with a loving but unrelenting eye. You will find the answer.

Whether you're dealing with a rebel teenage child, a jealousy issue with a sibling, a mother–daughter conflict, a neighbour dispute, a workplace disagreement or going through a contentious divorce, it's all the same challenge. We're different, and relationships are tough. Love is the only salve that heals, acceptance the only tool that mends and forgiveness, compassion and tolerance the only path to peace. If you make a commitment to any relationship, casual or deep, you are offering a part of yourself.

I wish you all love, for what else could I offer you that is more important or valuable? But I want you to feel love inside yourself first then it will be reflected in all your outward dealings. Love too is infinite; you can never run out of it and no one will ever love you more or better than you can love yourself.

Remember, vibes are contagious, both the good and the bad ones!

Use that as your foundation for all relationships and you can't go wrong.

References

Bradshaw, John 1992, *The Homecoming*, Bantam, New York.
Broder, Michael 1988, *The Art of Living Single*, Wilkinson Books, Australia.
Coelho, Paulo 1994, *The Alchemist*, Harper, San Francisco.
Dyer, Wayne 1992, *Real Magic*, HarperCollins, Australia.
Gawain, Shakti 1982, *Creative Visualisation*, Bantam Books, New York.
Hay, Louise 1984, *You Can Heal Your Life*, Hay House, Carlsbad, CA.
Gray, John 1996, *Men, Women and Relationships*, Hodder Headline, Sydney.
Montgomery, Bob and Evans, Lynette 1983, *Living and Loving Together*, Penguin, Harmondsworth.
Jeffers, Susan 1992, *Dare to Connect*, Random House, Sydney.
Lee, John 1990, *Facing the Fire*, Bantam Books, New York.
Ray, Sondra 1976, *I Deserve Love*, Celestial Arts Publishing, Berkeley, CA.
Redfield, James 1994, *The Celestine Prophecy*, Bantam Books, Sydney.
Rowland, Michael 1993, *Absolute Happiness*, A Self-communication book, Hay House, Carlsbad, CA.
Saunders, Charmaine 1998, *Women and Stress*, HarperCollins, Melbourne.

—— 1997, *Men and Stress*, HarperCollins, Melbourne.
—— 1997, *Teenagers and Stress*, HarperCollins, Melbourne, 1997.
Scovel-Shin, Florence 1986, *The Game of Life*, Simon and Schuster, New York.